THE BUSINESS OF PAINTING

A manual to show the ambitious painter who wishes to start his own painting business how to do it successfully.

BY

ARTHUR COLE

Latest Revision; April 2016

ISBN: 147017135X

ISBN 13: 9781470171353

ACKNOWLEDGEMENTS

Alfonso Puccio, my accountant: He prevented me from dispensing errors in the chapter on accounting, but more important, he gave me sound advice and direction through many years of mistake -making on my part. He taught me the value of honesty in business dealings.

Natale Santora: He saved my business skin at a time of financial disaster, by continuing to sell to me on credit when no "bottom line only" creditor would have done so. He enabled me to pull out of a situation of negative net worth and regain my business' strength.

Philip Lizotte: My business partner in the sixties, who taught me the value of concentration on business at a time when I was distracted by a myriad of unrelated goals.

Barbara Cole: My wife/partner who suffered through years of my experimentation with all kinds of approaches to business until we finally found our niche

AUTHOR'S PROLOGUE

I began putting this book on paper while I was still running my business and I dragged it out for several years. By the time I was finished I had been retired for ten or more years. That turtle-like speed explains why some of the pay scales and material prices I have used as examples may seem quaintly low to you. If they do, don't worry that they might make the whole book an obsolete instrument of an old fogy's failing memory. They don't.

The reason that they don't is that all the principles that I describe are true and useful **no matter what the economy may do to prices.**

Every once in a while I browse this book to see if any improvements are needed. Sometimes they pop up because changes keep happening in respect to tools, technology, improved methods of advertising etc. The most recent previous edition was created in 2015. This revision may well turn out to be my last because I am now 87 years old.

The painting business that I founded in 1957 is still thriving under the name Arthur Cole Painting Corp. Two of my kids now own and manage it. Its website's URL is cole painting .com. Check it out.

Arthur Cole

TABLE OF CONTENTS

INDEX OF ILLUSTRATIONS

CHAPTER ONE

WHY ENTER THE PAINTING BUSINESS?

Good question. Did you ever notice that any time a bum, vagrant, hippie, hobo, or tramp, if he becomes newsworthy for any reason, is labeled by the news media "an unemployed painter"? It took me years to figure out why that was, and I finally concluded that anyone who has ever dipped a brush into a liquid and spread it on a board thinks he can qualify as a painter. Nearly everyone has been employed for at least one half hour in his lifetime to paint something, so, in the eyes of America's public, that experience allows him to call himself a painter. No matter that nobody has the effrontery to call himself an electrician if he has screwed in a light bulb or a plumber if he has unplugged a sink trap; anyone can still define himself a painter in this country and get away with it. It probably has something to do with the "Do-it-yourself" movement created by the merchandisers of building products. Painting LOOKS easy even if it is not.

So why should a professional painter go into competition with all the amateurs? The answer is; he shouldn't! Leave the junk jobs to the amateurs. If you wish to be a painting contractor, do the kind of work the amateurs cannot do. You can't compete with them anyway (in terms of price) and you demean yourself by trying. Jesus is quoted in the Bible by one of his disciples as saying something to the effect that the poor will always be with us. We could amend that to say that poor workmanship will always be with us. Ignore the competition of those who produce schlock and stick to producing quality work on your jobs.

This book makes no pretense of teaching you the trade. It assumes that you all ready know it. Its purpose is to enable the accomplished painter to do it as a business rather than as an employee of someone else's business.

It is difficult to accumulate great wealth in the painting business but not impossible. I would be the last person to recommend it for "getting rich". I do, however, recommend it to professional painters as a way of life which can bring great satisfaction, a stable income, and pride of accomplishment. If you remember not to compete with the rabble you will enjoy the prestige and financial security you earn.

The painting business has some excellent long-term advantages over other businesses. For example, it is relatively free from the disasters which befall other businesses in times of recession. This is not to say that it is recession-proof, for it is not. Rather, it does not die out when public tastes change, as restaurants and retail stores sometimes do. In fact, it is enhanced by changes in public taste because the public wants color changes. It does not die out when industrial plant expansion slows down, because existing structures still have to be maintained, and painting is a major part of maintenance.

The painting business is fun. You meet new and fascinating people every week, and work in new and different buildings every week. Compare that stimulation to a life stuck at one machine in a factory or one desk in a cubicle in front of one computer terminal.

Who should go into the business? I will answer this question after first saying that the "you" I refer to can be either an individual or a partnership of two or three people. Certain skills are necessary and the "you" must have them all. In a partnership, each partner does not need to possess all of these skills but the partnership as a team must possess them all. These skills are;

1. **A thorough knowledge of the trade.** You must have several years of experience in most but not necessarily all phases of the trade. An apprenticeship under master painters is extremely helpful but not absolutely necessary. If you lack thorough knowledge, delay entering the business until you have achieved it.

2. **An open, inquiring mind**, eager to learn more and more and more.

3. **A clear understanding of arithmetic, simple algebra, and geometry**. This is necessary for purposes of cost estimating and record keeping.

4. **A willingness to keep clear and accurate records.** Business records provide you with information, and information is the lifeblood of any business. A shirt pocket filled with scraps of paper will simply not do.

5. **Literacy to a level higher than just high school**. You will have to read and understand contracts, insurance documents, architectural specifications, government regulations and on and on. If you have a liberal college education don't think it is a waste. It will forever be very useful.

6. **Honesty.**

7. **In a partnership, a willingness to discuss all issues openly with each other.** Since most partnerships are originally based on a mutual admiration, it is difficult to find fault with your partner. But if he or she is doing something you believe is harmful to the business, you must discuss and resolve the problem.

8. **At least one of the team of "you" must be computer literate.** No business can survive without such skill. It would be best if the owner(s) qualified for this require-ment. The only way that a painting contracting company can survive without such built-in skill would be to hire an employee who can fill that slot. The employee choice is risky though, because the owner(s) without computer literacy would be unable to recognize any weakness in the employee's skill level and honesty.

Who should not go into the painting business (or any business, for that matter)?

1. **The true believer.** In other words, the redneck, Nazi, Communist, religious fanatic, or anyone else whose political philosophy is so overweening that all his actions in life are ruled by it. Such a person cannot succeed in business because his attitudes will drive away custom-ers.

2. **The con artist** should not go into painting. He will be found out and ostracized long before he makes his big hit and moves on. Painting simply does not lead to the quick buck. More fertile fields are available to the con man. County government, for example.

3. **The late riser**. You have to be up early and in the shop to organize your day's work early. For one thing, you need

to know what to expect from the weather for your outside work, but mainly because your employees have to be on the job early and getting them off on time always seems to take last minute organizing.

If these simple rules do not scare you away, read on.

I mentioned honesty earlier as a requisite character feature for anyone in this business or any business. I did not elaborate then but I will now.

The first rule to follow is the advice of Socrates. KNOW THYSELF. You must examine yourself objectively at all times. If you understand what motivates you, you will be able to understand others also. For example, let us suppose that you have a job to do for a highly valued customer who gives you lots of repeat business, and the job goes well and you find yourself making far more profit than you planned on. Suddenly, the idea pops into your head to charge the customer less than the agreed contract price. Before taking that action you should ask yourself; 1. Am I doing this because I want to be liked? 2. Am I doing this because I fear losing this customer to the competition? 3. Will this gift cause the customer to look more favorably on my service and enhance his loyalty? 4. Will the customer, on the other hand, think he was being gouged in the first place and wonder why I am making such big profits at his expense? If you answer these questions honestly, you can then easily answer the question, would it be a wise decision to give your customer a price reduction?

A business person's greatest asset is his reputation. If suppliers do not trust you to pay them they will not give you credit. If customers do not trust you to do the job contracted for, they will not hire you. If banks do not trust you they will not lend money, and if your employees do not trust you they will sabotage your jobs. Most important of all, if you have a partner, he or she must trust you completely. The easiest way to keep your partner's full trust is to keep him fully informed on what you are doing at all times. Failure to inform can appear to be secrecy even if it is not. Marriages and business partnerships are alike in that secrecy can ruin them. Who knows, you could even be married to your partner.

What should you name your business? First look at a few rules on what NOT to name your business.

1. **Funny, cute, catchy, or gimmicky names**. Never call your business anything like "The Jolly Daubers". People will fear to do business with you. They will expect sloppy, carefree clowns, not professional painters.

2. **Names that imply that you are a fool**. I once saw a truck bearing the logo "Low Bid Construction Company". Such a name proves that you are an idiot.

3. **Meaningless names**. Too many businesses use monikers like Acme, Superior, Apex, Southwestern, New England, Paragon and so forth. These names may not be bad but they are not good. They mean nothing.

4. **Acronyms** like BESST Painting or combinations of first names like Jofred for Joseph Somebody and Frederick Somebody who are partners.

These names are trivial and petty. Your business might outgrow the name and need to change it later in order to be taken seriously by the customers. General Motors would never have grown as big as it has if its name had forever remained "Willie's Garage"

What is left? Your name. Your names, if you have partners. When a potential customer calls you on the telephone, he is pleased to talk to a person whose name is on the logo. He will never ask for Mr. Acme, Mr. Low Bid or Mr. Jofred. He wants you! Let your personal reputation enhance that of your business and vice versa. The only exception I can think of to this solid rule is that your name may be too difficult. If it is unpronounceable or has too many syllables or too many consonants, you might wish to use another name. A name picked out of a hat may be better than one that tangles tongues. Any American can say "John Adams" but very few can say "Taddeuscz Szlyck".

CHAPTER TWO

KNOWING YOUR CUSTOMERS

Many kinds of people inhabit this world, and as a business-man you will have to deal with them. To do so successfully, follow this rule:

KNOW YOUR CUSTOMER'S MOTIVATION. If you know what drives a person, you will know how to please him or, at least, avoid displeasing him. Before I learned this rule I lost a lot of business by misunderstanding what different custom-ers wanted. Customers will often fail to make clear to you what they want, so sometimes you will have to keep them talking until you really understand their goals.

Here are some types of customers whom painting con-tractors often encounter.

1. THE MERCHANT. A merchant is a person who buys goods at wholesale and sells them at retail. His income derives from the difference between the two prices (wholesale and retail) less his cost of doing business (overhead). There are only a few basic motivations that drive his busi-ness decisions. He does not create something of eternal value in the way that a music arranger, an architect, or a machine designer does. Yet, most people are creative in some way, or at least want to be. The merchant has only three outlets for his creativity. The first is his tal-ent for spotting an untapped market and filling it. Great

merchants such as Filene, Ward, Walton, and Woolworth had and used that talent. The second outlet, inventing better sales techniques, is the domain of second level merchants. Notice how automobile salespeople operate some day. It's a real eye opener. The third outlet, used by all merchants is finding ways to reduce overhead without hurting sales. Since they all think a lot about reducing overhead, expect them, when they consider painting, to think cheap. A merchant wants to maximize the effect of painting work while minimizing the cost. He is not interested in long term building maintenance. He wants IMMEDIATE EFFECT. He knows his customers will not give a fig about the quality of finishes in his store. His customers want selection, quality, price, and service in a surrounding congenial to that end. They scrutinize his goods, not his space. He, therefore, wants painting done ONLY AS NEEDED TO ENHANCE SALES. Your willingness to perform your work without interfering with his sales and your ability to do it without damage to his stock in trade are what he wants and what you must supply in order to sell your services to the merchant. Forget about sanding the woodwork to a furniture finish. He won't pay for it. He wants good service and low price only.

2. THE SHORT TERM REAL ESTATE DEVELOPER. There are two types of short term developers. One type buys land, builds housing, and sells it. The other buys land, builds commercial property, and rents it. In reality, these people are merchants in that they share the same basic motivations as wholesale-retail sellers of goods. The difference is that they actually own the real estate on which you, as a painting contractor, wish to work. The house builder knows that houses built on speculation will bring a cer-

tain price at the time of sale. He knows that he cannot get more than the public will pay, so the only way he can make a profit is to produce a saleable product at a cost which is lower than the selling price. Thus, cost control is the speculative builder's area of creative concentration. Using his knowledge of construction costs and market demand, he designs houses that will sell above cost. He rarely hires architects because they cost money that he believes can better be spent elsewhere or not spent at all. (This may explain the abundance of architectural monstrosities in suburban America). At any rate, the house builder, like the retailer, has a vested interest in keeping costs down. He also knows that the house buying public cares little or nothing about quality painting. Therefore, he usually hires amateurs if he is a small scale builder, or foolish painting contractors who give away their labor at less than cost, if he builds on a large scale. (To avoid becoming a foolish painting contractor who gives away labor at less than cost, see chapter 11 which will teach you how to know what your labor is costing you.)

The house builder's motive is cost control first and satisfactory cosmetics second. Long term maintenance and quality work are meaningless to him.

The short term real estate developer who builds and rents commercial property has the same goals only slightly modified. Since he keeps the buildings for fifteen or twenty years, he has to keep them looking presentable for that long to maximize profit when he sells out. Maintenance is in his budget but it is short term, low cost maintenance. Don't suggest that he sandblast his exterior steel columns to near white metal and coat them with epoxy. All he wants you to do is sand the rusty spots, spot prime, and slap on another coat of alkyd.

When the short term developer builds a commercial building he does it cheaply. Most shopping centers, strip malls, and motels are built this way. Their planned economic life is only twenty five or thirty years. Knowing that, you can tailor your proposals to fit the owner's desires. If you can suggest a way for him to achieve his desired result at lower cost he will listen to you. It will boost your chance of getting the job.

3. THE LONG TERM REAL ESTATE DEVELOPER. This person (or corporation, more likely) builds downtown commercial buildings in cities and keeps them indefinitely for rental income. All skyscrapers are built to high standards of public safety, which cost a lot, and most are built to high standards of finish. First class office space requires high quality painting work and the managers of first class real estate know how to recognize it. The primary motive of these managers of permanent buildings is to keep the space rented at high rents. To do that, they must seek as tenants companies such as law firms, accounting firms, stock brokerages, etc. whose own clienteles expect them to occupy lavishly appointed space. If they can fill their buildings with long term tenants of this character, they are contented.

The quality building manager, therefore, needs from you, his favorite painting contractor, quality work, service on schedule, and a fair price, in that order of importance. Notice I did not say a LOW price! Don't even try to compete for this business on the basis of price. Sell yourself on your quality work and good service.

4. INSTITUTIONS. By institutions I mean universities, main line churches, museums, symphony halls, and libraries. By nature, these buildings are expected to last as long as the institutions they house; that is, forever. Even if the buildings in question are not really good enough to last forever, the institutions that own them usually treat them as though they will. (The only exception I can think of is college dormitories which are realistically expected by their owners to be annually trashed by their occupants). The managers in charge of maintenance of institutional buildings are motivated by quality, service, and fair price with price being a minor consideration. By far the strongest motivation for these people is quality. If you ever had trouble satisfying a housewife on a color match, try satisfying an art museum! We once spent a whole week trying to mix certain colors demanded by a museum curator for use in one gallery. She could see nuances of color that my eyes could not see (or, at least she said she could, and I had to please her).

5. HOMEOWNERS. Homeowners with small incomes will never hire you, so forget them. They always do their own painting or leave it undone entirely. Homeowners with large incomes, however, are a potential market. It is difficult to classify them by motives, however, because their occupations and backgrounds define the way they think. The fact that they own their own homes is irrelevant. One type is the homeowner with generations of inherited wealth. This person is more like an institution in his attitudes than like a merchant. (Some of them even think of themselves as institutions One of my residential painting customers was a direct descendent of a United States president).

You should talk to them on the level of quality and service. Price tends to be a minor consideration. The wealthy homeowners whose incomes are earned by them and not by their ancestors are more diverse in their motives. For example, a divorce lawyer spends his every working day placing a dollar value on things which really cannot be measured in dollars. But he does it anyway because that is his job. Negotiation is in his blood. If your homeowner-customer is a divorce lawyer, he will just naturally try to beat you out of something, so plan for it in advance. A merchant, as described before, will look at the cost of residential painting as a cost to be reduced. So plan on it. Let him win a little in negotiations and he will be happy. A happy customer is good to have.

6. CORROSION ENGINEERS. These people do nothing but think about corrosion and ways to defeat it. Protective coating work is a lucrative field for a painting contractor but only if he knows what he is talking about. Never try to convince a corrosion engineer that flat latex is as good as any other paint on steel submerged in salt water. If you wish to enter this field and need to gain knowledge, join the SSPC (Steel Structures Painting Council). Its articles and seminars are very valuable. Also get to know one or two sales representatives from the major manufacturers of specialized coatings. These people are usually experts who will help you help your customer decide what system to use for his particular problem. They are salesmen, to be sure, but they represent paint manufacturers who want to satisfy engineers, not merchants. Thus, they would be no good to their employers if they did not know corrosion control from A to Z. If an engineer customer requests your help in

solving a corrosion problem, for heaven's sake do not bluff if you do not know the answer. Tell him you would like to consult with a specialist before making a recommendation. Then run to a phone and call your favorite salesman. If he does not know the answer, the corrosion engineers at his factory will. Nobody knows more about what products to use than those who make them.

Your engineer-customer wants results, not bravado. His driving motive is results and results only. To him, cost is not a major consideration because he compares it with the much greater cost of not painting. If you take his problem seriously, he will take you seriously as his contractor.

7. DECORATORS. Decorators differ from engineers. Antarctica and the Amazon basin are equally different. Decorators are alternately delightful, appalling, outrageous, and brilliant. They are never boring. A decorator has two basic motives, which are (1) to create and (2) to profit by it. Most decorators earn their income from profit on the direct sale of products to the owner, or from commissions on the sale of products by other suppliers. Therefore, it is in the decorator's interest to have the customer select expensive carpets, furniture, drapery, and wall coverings.

The decorator has no interest in economizing, so don't talk price to the decorator. If you must talk to him or her at all, discuss colors and textures and nice stuff like that. Do not mention price.

Decorators like to use trendy words to describe eternal verities such as color. I once had a job of painting, wood finishing, and paperhanging in an office suite about to be occupied by a law firm. My customer was the general contractor doing the renovations, but the tenant (the law firm) had hired a decorator. He was an elegant fellow. He had selected an obscenely expensive wallpaper to use in the large general office. It had an umber gray background with erratic streamers of several colors squirming on it in a random pattern. One of those colors was a yellow-green. During a conversation about mixing paint to match one of the colors in the paper I asked him, "do you mean that pea soup green?" The decorator elbowed me in the ribs and hissed from the side of his mouth, "At these prices it's called TAUPE!" We both had a good laugh and to be perfectly fair to him, the lawyer customer was not present and the warning was made in jest, but it does illustrate where the decorator was "coming from".

8. BUREAUCRATS. When painting bids are let out on public buildings, most awarding authorities are required by law to write specifications very carefully so that no ambiguity can creep in. They even tell you exactly how much you must pay your employees per hour in most states. This is so that every bidder is bidding on exactly the same thing. If the specification writer is completely successful in this endeavor, no potential bidder will need to request any clarification. When bids are taken, the awarding authority rejects any that are qualified in any way by the bidder, again so as to be sure that all bidders are bidding on the same work. In most cases, then, the job is awarded to the lowest bidder automatically so as to avoid political favoritism. So, if you decide to bid on public work, and the above described conditions pertain to your state and city, then you must read the specifications with the same care that the bureaucrat wrote

them. If you get the job he will expect you to do it the way the specifications require. This may sound like a situation in which the only variable in bid prices will come from variations in quality of workmanship, but this is not always true. I recommend that you read the specifications with such care that you may find something the writer should have said but did not. For example, you may find that, if it is a job with several trades working under a general contractor, that the general contractor is required to provide staging for you, and that requirement is in HIS specifications, not yours. Careful reading can sometimes provide you with a competitive edge. The only other way to get a competitive edge is in the efficiency of your crew. In other words, PRODUCTIVITY. Naturally, productivity is something you always have to think about. Productivity is the product of good tradespeople and this book presupposes that you already have that skill and knowledge. If you do not, close this book and read no further. The business of painting is not for you. Except for bureaucrats, customers' motives are not on display. They often do not know themselves what motivates them. Therefore, you have to figure them out for yourself so you will know how to deal with them.

This should help.

CHAPTER THREE

OPERATING POLICIES
······································

It is important to think out how you want to operate in advance of starting a business. In the business of painting there are several different types of work and not everyone is equally qualified to do all of them. They are;

1. Cost estimating

2. Organizing and supervising the actual work done by your painters

3. Sales and contract negotiation

4. Administration of the business office

In a very small business, one owner might be required to do them all, but he can, at least, hire certain skills he may not possess on his own, if only on a part time basis. We will examine these skills in chapter 16 but first let me recommend some policies to adopt and follow. By doing so, you can write rules for yourself and your employees to follow and thus create a corporate culture. Don't laugh. You may not have noticed it, but every corporation that succeeds has its own approach to business and its own attitudes toward suppliers, customers, employees, and the general public. These add up to its corporate culture. Starting a new business gives you the chance to build a corporate culture shaped in the image of your personal ideas. Heady, isn't it?

I recommend that you have a policy on priority of payments to creditors. We all know that the amount of cash in the checking account is never enough to pay all the bills that are waiting to be paid. Thus, when there is money available to be paid out, some creditors must have a higher priority than others. I suggest the following priority schedule, running from highest to lowest.

1. **Payroll**. This is obvious. Federal labor law requires that employees be paid on payday. If your regular pay period is a week, then you cannot make your employees wait more than seven days from the end of the pay period until they get paid and that payday has to be the same day each week. Most businesses pay wages only two or three days after the close of the pay period and you will find that new employees will be accustomed to that practice from their former places of employment.

2. **Governments**. Money you have withheld from employees for taxes, social security, etc. plus your share of social security contributions, and premiums to the state and federal governments for unemployment insurance all must be paid when scheduled to be paid. State and federal taxes on your company's income should also be promptly paid. Since governments have a lot more power than you have, they can make it difficult and miserable for you if you do not.

3. **Subcontractors**. Subcontractors working for you are supplying labor, which has to be paid each payday the same as yours does. If you want good service and workmanship from subcontractors, then cultivate their loyalty by paying them as soon as possible. Subs can make you look either very good or very bad to your customer, so make them loyal to you with prompt payments.

4. **Suppliers**. Most of your suppliers will be paint dealers. They too want prompt payment but they are realistic enough to know that direct labor, government, and sub-contract labor must hold higher priority on your payment list than they do. If a supplier calls you requesting a payment, NEVER promise a payment you cannot make. ALWAYS level with him. Tell him that you pay the oldest unpaid invoices first whenever you have money available to pay to suppliers and stick with that policy. Once they get to know you they will begin to trust you. Trust is your most important asset.

5. **Your banker**. Surely, somewhere along the line you will have borrowed money from a bank for working capital. It is wise to pay off short-term notes whenever possible in order to avoid unnecessary interest charges. However, remember that the banker wants to lend you money. He is happy to have your loan account because his business is lending money. As long as your business is solvent, he does not want repayment.

I further recommend adoption of some more policies, such as;

1. Complain about a person's behavior when necessary but never malign his character. Let's look at a few examples. A painter in your employ borrows money from your business for an emergency and agrees to repay the loan through a series of payroll deductions over a few weeks. His ignorance of federal tax law leads him to think that taxes withheld from his pay should be lower than usual because his take-home pay is lower (because of the scheduled repayments). You attempt to convince him that the withholdings are correct but he cannot or will not understand. Normally that would be the end

of the problem because you control the money, but, in this case the employee tells all his co-workers that you are cheating him. Some of them believe him and company morale takes a dive. Your response could be to denounce him as a liar (which attacks his character) or order him to stop making the false allegation (which attacks only a specific case of misbehavior). To malign a person's character degrades and insults him. It says, in effect, that he is no good. If you do this you create an enemy. You don't need enemies, especially enemies in your employ. In this case you can legitimately threaten to fire him for libeling you if he does not agree to stop. If he agrees, he ceases his subversive activity and keeps his job, and company morale returns to normal. If he refuses, you fire him and company morale returns to normal. Either way, you uphold the principle of fair play and avoid making an enemy.

Another example. A general contractor has hired you to be his painting subcontractor on a complex job. This contractor's reputation for quality work is high and you expect to be held to high standards of workmanship and have priced the job accordingly. However you find that your customer's job superintendent is a fanatic. He wants you to power sand paint spots off plywood subflooring before carpets are laid. He wants you to paint water pipes inside cabinets where they are invisible. He wants you to sand exterior wood trim between coats on a cupola thirty feet above the ground. You consider none of these demands to be reasonable or required by your contract. You have two choices. You can tell him so and request that he desist from such nonsense (complain of a specific behavior) or call him a "subkiller" (attack his character). If you do the former and his behavior toward you does not change, then go over his head to his boss and restate the complaint. If you do the latter and attack his character you acquire an enemy. And, an enemy whose company owes you money is a bad thing to acquire.

One more example. Most of your painters are men but you do have some women on the payroll. One of the men resents the competition from women in what he considers "men's work". He consciously or subconsciously harasses, ridicules, and insults the women on a regular basis. This hurts the morale of the women, naturally, but it also hurts the morale of some of the other men who dislike his behavior but accept it for reasons of their own and keep quiet. You fear low morale among your employees and you observe what is going on. You have two choices. Call him a "male chauvinist pig" (attack his character) or order him to cease the anti-female activity and treat the women as his equals in the trade (modify his behavior). You have the carrot and the stick in the form of further employment of the offending guy or firing him, because his action is not only morale-depressing but it is also illegal.

So, remember. It is behavior that has to be corrected, not character. You cannot change a person's character but you can demand reasonable standards of behavior. Do it. It will become part of your corporate culture of which you and all your employees will be proud.

2. Do everything legally. This may sound over-simplistic but it needs saying nevertheless. Many contractors, because of desperation, find themselves tempted to go around the law. They fail to turn in their withholdings for lack of cash on hand. They fail to pay the posted wage scale required by law on some public jobs because they think they cannot compete if they do. They dump hazardous waste illegally because they find themselves

stuck with some and with insufficient money to get rid of it safely and legally. All of these impediments to operating legally can be avoided with good cost control. When you reach chapter 11 you will see cost control and overhead explained. The best thing about operating legally is the absence of fear of getting caught.

3. Honor all your contracts, including those with your insurers as well as those with your customers and sub-contractors. It is easy to think of big, bad, impersonal insurance companies as a prime target for a little cheating. Don't be tempted. Some day you will need performance bonding and those bonds come from insurance companies.

4. Guarantee your work. This is nowhere near as risky as it sounds because your guarantee is based upon the specifications provided by the owner in the first place. Thus, if you are hired to repaint the exterior of an 18th century wooden building, the owner has to know in advance that the remaining old paint will contain lead. He has to know, therefore, that chemical stripping, sanding, or burning to remove the old paint will have to be done under government supervision and with government permission. He has to accept whatever legal requirements and liability are required by the Environmental Protection Agency and/or the related state agency. He cannot delegate that responsibility to you unless you are licensed to do the work and accept the responsibility in writing. If your job is merely to scrape off loose paint, spot prime bare surfaces, and repaint over the old paint, then if more old paint comes loose from the clapboards nine months after you leave the job, and carries away your new paint with it, then you are not required

under your guarantee to repair it. On the other hand, if the old paint remains firmly adhered to the building but your new coat peels off of the old paint, then you are responsible and must make good. That, however, is easy to avoid if you know the trade and do your work carefully. If, on another job, you sign a contract to make the exterior of a building "leak free", you are leaving yourself wide open for damages because, even though you may make it water leak free from rain, you can never guarantee that high wind or flood will not cause the walls to leak air or water. You can never make a building air leak free. So, be careful of the words you sign.

Painting is sometimes done for cosmetic reasons only. When that is the case, try not to agree to any specific number of coats of paint. Often one coat will do the job just fine, but if you agree to apply two or three coats, then the owner has the right to expect them. When painting is done for protection of the substrate and the owner specifies sand blasting and one coat of passivator followed by three coats of aliphatic urethane, then do it. If you don't, and the coating fails, it is easy for a coatings engineer to prove that you are at fault and make you do the entire process over again for nothing.

If a customer's paint fails, do not immediately agree to honor your guarantee. Investigate carefully before doing so. It may not be your fault. We once did the painting on a new schoolhouse in which we painted hundreds of hollow metal doors with semi-gloss enamel. After all the other trades and we were finished, the general contractor began the final cleaning of the building before turning it over to the town. One of its laborers cleaned scuff marks off the doors with a rag soaked in lacquer thinner. Naturally, every spot his rag touched turned flat. We were easily able to avoid repainting all those doors at our own expense because we learned what had been done and escaped liability.

5. Never start a job until you have it clear in your mind what your customer wants. Customers are often unclear themselves so you sometimes have to lead them through a verbal questionnaire. Take the time to do it. After you have committed time and money to the project it is too late to find out what the customer's goals really are. We were once hired to repaint a steel tower in a large gravel pit. The tower's function was the separation of bank gravel into its various sized stones and to wash out its fine dust. Bank gravel would be carried by conveyor belt to the tower's top, from which it would descend by gravity through a series of rotating filters which separated it into finer and finer sizes of stone and simultaneously washed it with voluminous quantities of water. Since the whole structure was made of steel, you can imagine the abrasion that gravel and water would produce. Our agreement was to pressure clean all surfaces, sandblast the worst rust, spot prime all bare steel, and apply one full coat of enamel. The work was done on Sundays at an agreed hourly rate. After we worked there for several weeks the owner confronted me with the complaint that the job was costing too much. That surprised me because I had no idea how much he thought was too much. I was concentrating on the quality of the work without knowing that there was a budget for the job. I should have cleared up that question before starting the work. If he had given me a budget to meet, I would have known that the job, from his viewpoint, was primarily for cosmetics. I was one chastened puppy, but I learned the lesson. Now you learn it. Before you start the work, know what your customer wants.

CHAPTER 4

RECORD KEEPING
·································

This chapter will discuss four types of records you will need for success in the business of painting. They are:

1. books (financial records)

2. payrolls

3. job costs

4. files you need

   Knowledge is the mother's milk of business. If you don't know what you are talking about, you cannot make intelligent, informed decisions. You can surely "fly by the seat of your pants" but you will crash if you do. I do not mean to imply that all intuition is garbage. To the contrary, intuition is very valuable but it alone will not do. You must have facts at your disposal. Business decisions rely on facts. Save the use of intuition for decisions involving people. For example, assume that you are interviewing a painter who has applied to you for a job. When you ask him for names, dates, and telephone numbers of previous employers and he tells you, "the most recent job was for cash strictly under the table for Joe (last name unknown) in Saskatoon, Saskatchewan and the next most recent died, and the third most recent is bankrupt, out of business, and hiding in Florida; you have my permission to let your intuition put its foot in the door.

Another example: You get invited to bid on a complex, outdoor, sewage treatment plant job. The invitation comes from a general contractor for whom you have never previously worked and who invariably uses the painting services of one of your competitors. The job is ready to start painting in one week even though the general contractor has been working there for a year. The job is in northern Minnesota and the month is November.

Ask yourself, what am I getting into? Why me now? Did another painter back out at the last minute? If so, why? Do not view every invitation to bid as a blessing. Some invitations are traps for the unwary.

BOOKKEEPING

Back to "mother's milk". First let's talk about financial records. You must have a standard bookkeeping and accounting system set up by an accountant and it must be an accrual system. Here is why.

There are two bookkeeping systems in general use; CASH systems and ACCRUAL systems. In a CASH system you record only cash which flows into and out of your checking account. Each payment is assigned to an account such as material, subcontract, small tool expense, rent, truck maintenance, legal fees, payroll, commissions, etc. etc. etc. Please notice that some of these accounts are direct job costs (payroll, material) and others are indirect costs (overhead). More on overhead later.

Each receipt is entered into the books only when you make a deposit to the checking account and each payment is recorded only when you write a check. This beguilingly simple method of bookkeeping, if adopted, will destroy your business because it does not tell you what you need to know, namely, "am I making any money?" The typical naive painter who starts his own business gets credit from a paint store, gets a few contracts, and accumulates unpaid bills which he intends to pay when he collects from his customer. If he has done the estimating and the direct labor himself, his checkbook shows no entries at all. He stuffs the accumulating invoices into a drawer and forgets them.

Then his customers begin paying and suddenly his books come to life because checkbook entries have been made. He gets excited. "Wow, look at all the money in the checking account!" He buys equipment he does not really need and cannot really afford because he does not know whether or not his business is profitable. His books have kept him in the dark.

An ACCRUAL system, on the other hand, works this way. You keep track of cash receipts and disbursements the same as you do in the cash system but you also keep two very important accounts besides cash. They are accounts payable and accounts receivable.

When you get a bill for paint you have purchased but not yet paid for, you record it in two accounts called "accounts payable" and "material". When you actually pay the bill, the entry goes in "cash" (reducing the amount of cash on hand) and "accounts payable" (reducing the debt). The charge to "material" remains in your books unchanged, telling you what you need to know about where the money went.

When you complete a job and send a bill to your customer, you enter it in "income" just if you had actually been paid, and in "accounts receivable" (telling you what money you can expect soon). When your customer pays, you enter the payment under "cash" (increasing the amount of cash in the account) and "accounts receivable" (decreasing the amount owed you). Notice that income remains in the books unchanged, telling you what you need to know (how much your business billed).

The accrual system keeps you informed at all times regardless of how good or bad your cash flow is. So, don't even THINK about using the cash system. Have your accountant set you up with an accrual system and let it work for you.

Each month, quarter, or year end this system will produce for you a statement of profit and loss (P&L). You decide how frequently you wish a statement but I recommend no less than four per year. You or your accountant has to report your payrolls to the federal and state governments each quarter anyway, so it is a convenient time to take stock.

A sample statement of profit and loss is shown on plate 20.

PLATE 20

YOUR BUSINESS NAME
STATEMENT OF INCOME FOR THE YEAR ENDING 12/31/1993

SALES		510,345
COST OF SALES (direct costs)		
Materials	100,766	
Subcontracts	34,907	
Direct Labor	189,789	
FICA (social security)	14,518	
State Unemployment Insurance	6,324	
Federal Unemployment Insurance	451	
Depreciation	4,288	
Workers' Compensation Insurance	19,587	
General Liability Insurance	3.010	
Equipment Rental	4,000	
TOTAL COST OF SALES		377,640
GROSS PROFIT		132,705
OPERATING EXPENSES (overhead)		
Officers' salaries	42,000	
FICA, officers	3,213	
Workers' Compensation, officers	2,033	
Motor Vehicle Insurance	2,900	
Health Insurance	6,933	
Profit Sharing	3,800	
Interest	4,122	
Motor Vehicle maintenance and fuel	2,746	
Shop and Office Rent	6.500	
Legal and Accounting Expense	3,100	
Telephone	1,247	
Advertising	2,884	
Equipment Maintenance	997	
Dues and Subscriptions	350	
Small Tool Expense	1,568	
Miscellaneous General Expense	16,756	
Hazardous Waste Removal	5,980	
TOTAL OPERATIONAL EXPENSES		104,245
NET PROFIT OR (LOSS)		28,460

Please turn to that now and follow along. First of all, notice the top and bottom lines. The top line (SALES) is the INCOME figure for the period from your books. The bottom line is your PROFIT. An interesting thing to do each year is divide the profit by the sales (income) and find out what your MARGIN of profit is. In this hypothetical case the margin is .05 or 5 percent. In this business a profit margin of 5% is good.

If you think it is inadequate, raise your prices and see if the customers will accept the increase.

Another interesting measure, is to divide the profit by the capital invested. That will give you a figure known as RETURN ON INVESTMENT. Later on this chapter will show you a BALANCE SHEET (plate 21), and part of the balance sheet is the money you have invested in your business. It is called the total of CAPITAL and RETAINED EARNINGS. Capital is your original investment and retained earnings are profits earned in previous years which you have let the business keep as working capital. If we assume that your original investment plus your retained earnings add up to the $28,460 in the bottom line of plate 20, then your return on investment is 100%. By comparison, you could put the same money into a savings bank and earn a return on investment of 3% or maybe only 1%. The choice is yours. However, you could easily lose all of your capital in business, so just be careful.

Now, follow down through the profit and loss statement (plate 20) as we discuss each item. We have all ready discussed sales, so move on to the direct costs. Materials, subcontracts, and labor are obviously costs of doing jobs for customers. If you did not have any jobs, these expenses would not be incurred. FICA (social security contributions), the two unemployment contributions, and the two insurance items are all tied to labor cost. They too would not be incurred if you had no jobs. Depreciation is the loss in value of your equipment by way of aging. This cost, in my opinion, ought to be listed below in the column of costs which are indirect but accountants like to place it here as a direct cost. I choose not to tackle the whole accounting establishment on this issue because one thing I know about accountants is that they know more than I do about accounting.

Equipment rental is a direct cost because it is the expense of renting equipment for a specific job. If you did not have the job you would not rent the equipment. An air compressor would obviously fit into this category but a leased company car would not. The leased car would be an indirect cost (overhead) and appear below the gross profit as an operating expense.

Gross profit, itself, is the difference between Sales (income) and the Total Cost of Sales.

Now let's run down the list of operating expenses. Officers' salaries are clearly overhead because we assume that the officers are working to earn those salaries by managing the business. If they were drawing salaries without working, or if they were drawing salaries that were too large for the size of the business to justify, then they put the business at risk of failure through a draining of its capital. If you own the business and appoint yourself as president, take a salary adequate to your needs and stick with it even if the company thrives. Leave the retained earnings in the business. This will make your banker confident in your business acumen and he will reward you with steadily increasing access to short term borrowed capital. Nothing makes a banker more nervous than to see the businessman who just borrowed $50,000 to finance a painting job and then drives up to the bank in a $50,000 car.

If your business is small enough to require some of the actual direct labor on jobs to be performed by the officers, then you need to know how much of the officers' pay should be direct cost and how much should be listed as operating expense. For details on how to record that information, see the next section of this chapter, entitled PAYROLLS.

The same split between overhead FICA for officers, and direct cost FICA for officers can be made easily and will be explained in chapter 11.

Workmen's compensation for officers is charged at a much lower rate than for painters for the obvious reason that office work is less dangerous than construction work. This item also can be easily split between direct and overhead costs. That will also be explained later in chapter 11, OVERHEAD.

The next two items (motor vehicle insurance and health insurance) are probably self-explanatory.

They are fixed overhead expenses that will be incurred no matter how little or how much you have in SALES.

Profit sharing is an operating expense all right and therefore must show up on your P&L statement but it is not overhead. It is a bonus given voluntarily to employees or a voluntarily distributed dividend to stockholders. It comes out of your company's profit, naturally, but since it is voluntary it cannot be considered an item of overhead. (It is, however, deductible from your business' income tax).

Interest is self-explanatory. My only comment on that is that you could decide to differentiate between long term and short term interest in your books. The rationale is that long term interest is paid for money borrowed for capital investments such as motor vehicles and expensive equipment which will last several years. That interest could, and probably should, be considered overhead. Whereas short-term interest is used to pay for job expenses in anticipation of your customer's payments to you. If you did not have the job to finance, you would not need to borrow short-term money. Later, when I guide you through plate 9, you will see how short term interest is used as variable overhead, not fixed overhead as is long term interest For now, ignore that issue.

The next six items need no further explanation, so look at "Dues and subscriptions". This is a small but very important cost of doing business. You need two things that are provided under this category. They are (1) knowledge of changes that are always taking place in the industry and (2) access to help from experts in the industry. These subjects will be discussed in detail in chapter 8.

Small tool expense is a major part of the cost of painting because the tools are expensive and they wear out very rapidly. Tools are not a capital investment that will last a long time like a truck, computer, or air compressor. They are a cost which varies with the volume of work you are doing. Some people think that small tools should be listed above the line as a direct cost of doing business. There is some merit to that idea but I believe it should be down here with indirect costs because of the following reasons. (1) Ladders of all types should be considered small tools because they get broken, worn out, lost, or stolen fairly rapidly, although they DO last for more than one job, unlike roller covers. If you buy a new forty foot extension ladder and use it for the first time on a job worth only $1,000 you obviously cannot charge the entire cost of that ladder to that one job. But you can spread out the cost of that ladder over the fiscal year by entering it into "small tool expense" below the line. (2) You might stockpile paint pots or brushes purchased in volume and not use them up for several months. That period in which you use them up may extend from one fiscal year into the next. So, take my word for it. Keep small tool expense where it is. In the future, if you buy small tools in great volume for future use, you can still expense them (write off the total cost in one fiscal year) but if you wish not to load up that fiscal year with too much small tool expense on you P&L STATEMENT, you can carry an inventory item for such tools as a short term asset on your BALANCE SHEET. See your accountant for details if you decide to do this. If you are just starting out in business, I suggest you forget that for the time being because it is not a business life or death matter.

Miscellaneous general expense is a necessary evil. You should use it as little as possible but you will definitely have to have an account in which to enter things that do not fit anywhere else, such as the basket of fruit you send to the hospitalized wife of an employee.

Finally. "Hazardous waste removal". This type of expense is significant and growing. You cannot easily charge it out as a direct expense because the waste comes in from various sources, including your own work in the shop, cleaning equipment. Your customers, of course, foot the bill for hazardous waste treatment as they do for all of your costs of doing business, but it is easier to keep it as an operating expense below the line than it would be to attempt to attribute it to individual jobs as a direct expense.

Obviously, the difference between the gross profit and the net profit is in your overhead. Overhead is measured on a P&L statement by the figure titled "Total operating expenses". These costs can make or break your business and must be watched at all times. More on that subject later in the chapter titled "Overhead".

The next important report you should get monthly or quarterly is the BALANCE SHEET. This is prepared by your accountant simultaneously with the P&L STATEMENT. It tells you the current value of your business. Plate 21 is a sample balance sheet for the same business and the same date as the P&L statement I showed you on plate 20

PLATE 21

BALANCE SHEET AS OF DECEMBER 31, 2011

ASSETS

CURRENT ASSETS

Cash	$ 6,123.65
Accounts Receivable	71,954.77
Work in Process	3,996.00
TOTAL	$ 82,074.42

FIXED ASSETS

Equipment	$ 20,675.00
Furniture and Fixtures	1,850.45
Motor Vehicles	23,053.06
Less Accumulated Depreciation	(12,371.00)
TOTAL	$ 33,207.51
TOTAL ASSETS	$ 115,281.93

LIABILITIES AND CAPITAL

CURRENT LIABILITIES

Accounts Payable	$ 33,671.98
Accrued Taxes and Expenses	3,456.00
Notes Payable	24,000.00
TOTAL	$61,127.98

CAPITAL

Common Stock 600 shares	$ 18,000.00
Retained Earnings	36,153.93
TOTAL	$ 54,153.95
TOTAL LIABILITIES AND CAPITAL	$ 115,281.93

47

Now let's run through this sample balance sheet the same way we did the P&L statement, item by item. Beginning at the top, you will see CURRENT ASSETS. These are <u>things of immediate value</u>. I define immediate value as those items normally being useable now or at least within 30 days. Theoretically you can expect your accounts receivable to be collected within 30 days and turned into cash. (Don't plan your business life around theories, however). Your work in process is work in which you have invested money but not yet billed to your customer. Since it is not billed yet, it does not show in your books as accounts receivable but it does show up as expenses like material and labor. In order to get a clear picture of how you are doing financially, you need to calculate the value of your work in process. Ignoring it leads to an underestimate of your profitability. Overestimating it leads to the opposite. See chapter 15 on how to estimate the value of your work in process. For now, forget it and continue with this review of the balance sheet.

FIXED ASSETS are things of long term value. Equipment, furniture, and motor vehicles do not wear out in 30 days. Thus they are fixed assets. These dollar figures represent their original cost. They accumulate from year to year as time goes on and you continue to buy equipment. Now do not start worrying about how to account for its physical depreciation. That is taken care of by the next line item, Accumulated depreciation. This negative dollar figure also accumulates from year to year. Thus the total of fixed assets is a realistic picture of what your fixed assets are worth. Whenever you buy a fixed asset, you and your accountant decide upon a term of depreciation. For example, you may purchase a new diesel powered air compressor which you can normally expect to last fifteen years. If its cost is $30,000 your depreciation will be $2,000 per year. On the other hand, a small electric powered airless paint pump can be expected to last perhaps two years, so your depreciation schedule would be based on that term. A $3,000 pump would depreciate at $1,500 per year.

CURRENT LIABILITIES are immediate obligations. That is, within 30 days. Theoretically you will pay your accounts payable within that time and will do the same with any short term bank notes you borrowed to run the jobs. This is theory only as you well may have surmised. If you are unable to pay your suppliers and subcontractors within the thirty days, the obligation remains in your books and it remains under CURRENT LIABILITIES. Your bank notes (borrowed money), also, may be written for 90 or 120 days but for convenience, these obligations are still called CURRENT LIABILITIES in accounting parlance.

Accrued taxes are tax liability which you have incurred but which do not show up in your books until such time as a BALANCE SHEET is prepared. For example, you may operate in a state that requires businesses to pay a certain fee to the state each year regardless of whether it makes or loses money. Such a fee may be payable only once a year, at the end of your fiscal year. If you have a BALANCE SHEET done quarterly, then one quarter of that state fee should show up as accrued taxes. Accrued expenses are such things as workmen's compensation insurance which is tied to payroll. Usually the premium for such insurance is prepaid in whole or in part and shows up as a current asset in your books. The premium is based on an estimate of your payroll for the upcoming year. If you underestimate the payroll, then you will accrue additional debt to the insurer. That additional debt is listed under Accrued Expenses. In our sample BALANCE SHEET the two items are combined into one called Accrued Taxes and Expenses.

There is such category as FIXED LIABILITIES. I did not show it on this sample balance sheet because it is not a good idea for a painting business to carry any. An example of a fixed liability is a thirty year real estate mortgage. In any thirty day period it does not get paid off, therefore it is fixed, not current. If you should decide to own your own real estate and locate your paint shop and office on it, set up the real estate as a separate business. Do not mix it with your painting business. If you do, you will have no way to know if either business is dragging the other down.

CAPITAL is simple. Common stock is your original investment and retained earnings are previous years' profits which you have let the business keep and use as working capital. If you are not incorporated the words "common stock" would not appear but the original investment would still be listed here on the BALANCE SHEET. Now, this is important. <u>The total of capital is the value of the business.</u> It is the sum of the original investment and the retained earnings.

Now notice that the total assets balance with the total of liabilities <u>and </u>capital. If you have a money-losing year and your assets shrink in value, your retained earnings will also shrink in exactly the same amount. This is because your retained earnings are profit. So, if you take a loss your profit is affected negatively. Now let us move on to ---

PAYROLLS

Payrolls and their deductions are an integral part of your bookkeeping system but they are such an important part of the system that they must be looked at separately. You can and should purchase a predesigned payroll check system rather than trying to devise a method of payroll record keeping on your own. It is possible to have a computerized business bookkeeping and payroll system which will write checks, but I'm going to assume that you will not be that sophisticated at first because you do not need to.

A typical hand written payroll system has a series of pre-printed and numbered blank payroll checks which are hitched together so they cannot get out of place. It will also have an individual payroll record card for each employee and officer. That card will be imprinted by way of carbon paper each time a payroll check is written. It records how much the person earned in the pay period, how much was deducted for FICA, taxes, and any other deductions. It also records, if the person is paid by the hour, how many hours he worked, his hourly pay scale, how many hours of overtime he worked, and how much he was paid for both straight time and overtime.

The payroll system will also provide a "payroll journal" for each pay period. That is a record of the gross pay, deductions, and net pay for all the people paid that day. The total net pay is entered into your checking account as a negative figure each payday. The deductions are entered into your books as current liabilities because you will have to pay them out to governments soon.

All of this is strictly bookkeeping which any bookkeeper, including you, can easily handle. If you make a mistake your accountant can easily correct it for you. All of this is stand-ard business practice. There are other payroll records which you need to keep, outside of the books, for your own use in keeping track of overhead costs and job costs. For these records, make up your own forms. To make it easy for you to get started you can copy mine and later amend them to suit your specific needs. Let's assume that your payday is weekly, as is most commonly the case. See plate 11 for an example of the weekly form needed for each worker.

PLATE 11

JOB NAME	SUN	MON	TUE	WED	THU	FRI	SAT	S/T HRS	O/T HRS	ALL HRS	$ COST
Smith		8	3	1				12		12	120.00
Jones				7	8			15		15	150.00
Newton						6		6		6	60.00
Abstract					2				2	2	30.00
Williams							3	2	1	3	35.00
no job (onph)			5					5		5	50.00
TOTALS		8	8	8	10	9		40	3	43	445.00

Notice that each day has been filled with the number of hours the employee worked that day and on which jobs he worked. At the end of each week, the hours are totaled for each job and a dollar value attributed to each job based upon hours worked. This particular hypothetical employee gets paid at a rate of $10 per hour. When he works over 40 hours in a week the overtime hours are paid him at $15 per hour (federal labor law).

As you can see, he worked on five separate jobs plus five hours doing something not attributable to any job, for a total of 43 hours.

The total number of hours worked (43 in this case) MUST agree with the hours recorded in your payroll journal. More on that later. The $445 total gross pay for this employee for this week must also agree with the payroll journal. Furthermore, the horizontal lines and the vertical columns must add up correctly and agree with each other. When you have done that, your record has "proved" and cannot be incorrect. You will be amazed at how often you will refer to these records and at how glad you will be to have them. On two occasions my payroll records saved me from serious losses by proving in court that my billing was correct. In another trial (in which we were being sued for water damage to a clothing store located one floor below the one in which we had been working), our payroll records proved that we had completed and left the job a week before the pipe broke that caused the damage. The moral of this tale is, keep good records !

The second and last non-bookkeeping payroll record you need is the WEEKLY PAYROLL RECAPITULATION SHEET. This record collates the job cost information from the INDIVIDUAL WEEKLY PAY RECORDS (plate 11) and shows you how each job is doing. Plate 16 below shows a sample .

PLATE 16

WEEKLY PAYROLL RECAP

WEEK ENDING _____

EMPLOYEE	HOURS WORKED	GROSS PAY	ONPH HRS.	ONPH $	EST'G HRS.	EST'G $	Smith job HOURS	Smith job $	Jones job HOURS	Jones job $	Newton job HOURS	Newton job$	Abstract job HOURS	Abstract job $	Williams job HOURS	Williams job $
Trainor, W	4	$600.00		$540.00	13	$162.50					23	$287.50	4	$60.00		
Jackson, F	40	$500.00	4	$50.00			12	$120.00	15	$150.00	6	$60.00	2	$30.00	3	$35.00
Ruiz, P	43	$445.00	5	$50.00			4.5	$58.50	14.5	$188.50	20	$260.00				
Nelson, H	39	$507.00													40	$480.00
Ricker, O	40	$480.00														
TOTALS	166	$2,532.00	9	$640.00	13	$162.50	16.5	$178.50	29.5	$338.50	49	$607.50	6	$90.00	43	$515.00

54

As you may have noticed, the total of 166 hours worked on all the jobs agrees with the total of 166 hours attributed to the employees individually. This is imperative. If you fail to have these two numbers agree, your records are suspect and will not hold up to scrutiny by the Internal Revenue Service, your insurance carrier, a court, or any other institution which has life threatening power over your business. Also, the grand total of dollars paid out in payroll that week (on this form) must agree with the payroll journal. The grand total on this form is found by adding the job column totals, adding them together, and making sure the total agrees with the dollar amount at the base of the gross pay column ($2,532 in this case).

Now you may have wondered why there are columns for "0NPH" (no job)" and EST'G (estimating). "No job" refers to non-productive time, such as time spent fixing a flat tire on a company vehicle, time spent in the office on managerial tasks, time spent cleaning and repairing equipment, and so forth. Every business has down time which cannot be attributed to any particular job. Some of it is done by employees who are normally doing direct productive work on the jobs, but most of it is usually done by people in management positions. In the sample recapitulation sheet, (plate 16 above) the employee named Trainor is the company owner and is occupied mostly with "no job" duties. Whether he is salaried or paid in wages makes no difference if he actually works with the tools on a job. If, as he does in this example (four hours on the Abstract job), his time in hours and the corresponding portion of his salary are entered in that job column. The balance of his salary goes in the "no job" column without any entry for hours. Mr. Trainor (or Ms. Trainor, as the case may be) may not normally work on a job at all. In such a case, no hours will be included in the recap for Trainor. The princi-

PLATE 18

WEEKLY   PAYROLL RECAP

WEEK ENDING _____

PAYROLL RECAPITULATION WEEK ENDING _____

EMPLOYEE	HOURS WORKED	GROSS PAY	ONPH HRS.	ONPH $	EST'G HRS.	EST'G $	Smith job HOURS	Smith job $	Jones job HOURS	Jones job $	Newton job HOURS	Newton job$	Abstract job HOURS	Abstract job $	Williams job HOURS	Williams job $
Trainor	40	$720.00	-2	-$36.00	26	$468.00							16	$288.00		
Jackson, F.	40	$500.00			26	$325.00							1	$12.50		
Ruiz, P.	43	$445.00	5	$50.00			12	$120.00			13	$162.50	2	$30.00	3	$35.00
Nelson, H.	39	$507.00					4.5	$58.50	15	$150.00	6	$60.00				
Ricker, O.	40	$480.00							14.5	$188.50	20	$260.00			40	$490.00
TOTALS	202	$2,652.00	3	$14.00	52	$793.00	16.5	$178.50	29.5	$338.50	39	$482.50	19	$330.50	43	$515.00

ple to remember is that hours are not recorded for salaried people UNLESS they spend hours in direct labor on the jobs. Those hours will be recorded.   Hours and their corresponding pay are used for keeping track of job costs, down time ("no job"), and estimating done by hourly wage employees.

Now, here is a scenario to blow your mind. Let's say that your salaried person works on jobs doing direct productive labor and he does it for over forty hours in one week.

Since he is salaried, he does not get overtime pay, so how do you enter it in the weekly payroll recap ? Simple. You divide his weekly salary by forty hours to establish his rate of pay per hour. Then you apply the correct number of hours and dollars to each job. If the money allocated to his labor on jobs adds up to more than he actually gets paid for his weekly salary, you enter a negative figure in the "no job" column in the amount needed to make the line add up to his salary. For example, if Trainor, whose salary is $600 (or $15 per hour), works 41 hours on jobs, then you enter negative $15 in the "no job" column on the Trainor line. See plate 18 below for an example.

Estimating is also a labor item not attributable to any particular job. It could be included in "no job" because it certainly is an overhead expense, not a direct job expense. However, being a nitpicker, I like to see it kept separate for reasons which will be explained in chapter 11(Overhead).

Estimating in the painting business is usually done by managers but occasionally it is wise to get the input of your workers on some estimates. In the example shown in plate 16 above, the employee named F. Jackson spent thirteen hours on estimating in that week.

plate 17 (blank form)

JOB_____REG. #_____C. S. PAGE____
SALES TAX EXEMPT #_____
COST PLUS_____CONTRACT_____CONTRACT PRICE
$_____

LABOR			SUBCONTRACT			MATERIAL		
date	am't	hrs.	date	name	am't	date	name	am't
		frd			frd			frd
	frd	frd			frd			frd

REQUISITIONS				PAYMENTS RECEIVED			
date	amount	date	amount	date	amount	date	amount

and plate 19 (sample)

JOB _Jones_____REG. #__3386_____C. S. PAGE_1
SALES TAX EXEMPT #_____
COST PLUS_____CONTRACT_x____CONTRACT PRICE
$_4,200_____

LABOR			SUBCONTRACT			MATERIAL		
date	am't	hrs.	date	name	am't	date	name	am't
		frd			frd			frd
6/15	612.00	51	6/18	Atlas Sand	2500.00	6/10	Glidden	38.92
6/22	48.00	3		Blasting				
	frd	frd			frd			frd
	660.00	54		—	2500.0			38.92

REQUISITIONS   PAYMENTS RECEIVED

date	amount	date	amount	date	amount	date	amout
7/10	4200.00			8/1	1450.00		
				8/10	2750.00		
					4200.00		

JOB COST RECORDS

It goes without saying that you need to know how each job is doing financially and the only way to know that is to keep job cost sheets and enter them promptly upon completion of each payroll. In the painting trade, labor is the greatest expense by far, so it is important to keep payroll entries up to date each week. Material purchases are not as significant and could be recorded on the cost sheets less frequently if you are hard pressed for time. Anyway, a simple but effective format for keeping job records is shown on

Please refer to plate 19. The header contains, beside job identification information, a space for you to use in numbering pages. Large jobs require multiple pages, so do not let yourself get mixed up by failing to number them. Just above the billing record space is a line for totals if it is a one-page record or page subtotals if it is a multi-page record. This sample shows a very small job, which used only 54 man-hours of labor, $660.00 in direct wages, $2500.00 in subcontract, and $38.92 worth of material. If it were a multi-page record you would transfer these numbers to the top of page two.

The billing and payment records usually will fit on one page of the cost record; therefore it makes sense to enter that information on page 1. In this sample, only one bill was sent and only two payments received, at which time the job was fully paid for. Big jobs will have many billing and receipt entries and it is useful to have a quick reference location for that information. This is the place.

While we are on the subject of billing, notice that the sample shows direct costs of $660.00 for labor, $2500.00 for subcontract, and $38.92 for material. Their total is $3198.92 and you billed the job at $4200.00.

This does not mean that the job made over $1,000 profit, though. That is because OVERHEAD is part of the cost and does not show on the front of the cost record. It shows up on the back of the cost record. That is where you recap an individual job and learn how much money the job made or lost. Now please refer to plate 14 below.

PLATE 14

JOB COST RECAP BASED ON OVERHEAD OF YEAR *1993*

Total Hours labor *54* X $ *7.67* (fixed overhead)	*414.18*
Total direct wages	*660.00*
Direct wages X *58%* (variable overhead)	*382.80*
Subcontract expense	*2500.00*
Material expense	*38.92*
TOTAL COST (SUM OF LINES ABOVE)	*3995.80*
Total Amount Billed	*4200.00*
NET PROFIT OR (LOSS)	*204.20*

This form should be printed on the back side of your job cost record form so that you can recap the job's financial performance in a place where it cannot be separated from the job's specific cost records. The sample shown here recaps the same job described above. Now you will learn if it made any money. Read on.

Fixed overhead is established as $7.67 per hour based on the most recent year in which you calculated it. Don't worry yet about how you got that number. It will be explained in chapter 11. Total direct wages is entered from the front of the cost sheet. The next item, variable overhead, is also explained in chapter 11. In this case it is 58% of direct wages. Trust me.

Subcontract is directly entered from the front of the cost record. The rest is simple arithmetic and voila, the job made money.

The purpose of this sample is to show you the way to arrive at a job profitability figure as closely as you can possibly get. The reason for the space at the top where you list what fiscal year you base your figures on, is that your overhead varies from year to year and it is best to use the most recent year on which you have available figures because that year will probably most closely resemble the year in which you are working. Now let's move on to something easier to absorb but equally important for getting you off to a good start.

FILES YOU WILL NEED.

In the first year you can probably get along with only two or three file drawers. A list of folders which must be established immediately here follows;

<u>A folder for each job</u>. This will keep all job related information together.

It will contain purchase orders, contracts, estimates, correspondence, color schedules and any other documents related to actually doing the job. When the job is complete and paid up you will add to the folder the paid up copies of bills you sent to the customer and the recapitulated cost record. The latter is often useful in helping you estimate future jobs in the same building. We have painted the interior of several churches and one antique concert hall twice and the exteriors of several buildings three or more times. Each time we record the number of man-hours used and this sure makes future estimating more accurate than it would be otherwise.

<u>Thirteen folders for uncontracted estimates</u>. Why thirteen, you ask ?

Because twelve of them will be labeled, January, February, and so on through December. Each month, place the estimates done that month in the month's folder and leave them there until such time as they are needed (like when you are awarded a job). Most contractors do a lot more estimates than they do jobs. You will too. After you have filled twelve monthly folders, at the start of each new month, go through the year old estimates in that folder and discard all but those estimates which still may be needed. Those you will file in the thirteenth folder, called "estimates over one year old". This folder won't get very fat so you can clean it out some rainy day in the future when you are bored and want to do some house cleaning.

<u>Invoices received</u>. When invoices from subcontractors and suppliers come in, someone has to review them and decide to what accounts to charge them . For example, an invoice contains a gallon of paint and a seventy five pound bale of paint rags. The gallon of paint will be entered in the books as material and the rags will be entered as small tools. When these decisions have been made, the invoice is now ready for actual bookkeeping entry but that may not be done the same day. So, the invoice is safe from getting lost, neatly tucked away in its folder along with all of its brother not-yet-entered invoices. In order to give clear instructions to the bookkeeper, have a rubber stamp made up to match the format shown on plate 22 below.

Stamp each incoming invoice with this stamp, check the invoice for correctness, and then fill in the upper portion of the stamp as follows;

PLATE 22

DATE RECEIVED_____

JOB_____ $_____

JOB_____ $_____

JOB_____ $_____

SMALL TOOLS $_____

OTHER ACC'T _____$_____

CHECKED BY_____AP#_____

COST SHEET ENTRY BY_____

PAID CHK #_____DATE_____

Date received is obvious. The next three lines all assume that they will be used for materials on certain jobs. The Small Tools line is for small tools, of course, and is very useful in this trade because we use up so many tools so quickly. Frequently nearly every invoice from a paint supplier will have both materials and small tools on it. Small tools is an overhead expense, not a direct expense. The Other Account space is for any other overhead account besides Small Tools. This could be Office Expense if you purchased cellophane tape, Equipment Maintenance if you bought penetrating oil, or Accounting and Legal if your lawyer sends you a bill. In the Checked By space place your own initials. When the bookkeeper enters the invoice into the business' accounts payable journal, he or she will then enter the page number of the journal in the space called AP#.

That gives you a cross reference from invoice to journal and vice versa and believe me, you will be glad you have it. "Cost Sheet Entry By" is initialed by the person who enters these job related expenses (material usually) in the job cost record (plate 17 above). The only reason for this entry is to make sure that the job cost sheet entry gets made and not forgotten.

Paid Invoices.   You need one drawer for these and one folder for each vendor from whom you buy anything regularly plus one folder for miscellaneous vendors.   File them alphabetically by vendor in their file drawer and chronologically in each vendor's folder. When you pay a vendor for a group of invoices, staple them together with the date paid and check number used in payment on the stamp space as described above. Internal Revenue Service rules require that you keep all business records at least seven years, so these folders can become obese. Folder obesity, however, is a small price to pay for good records.

Invoices Entered and Unpaid.   After incoming invoices are entered into the books and into the job cost records, put them into this folder alphabetically by vendor's name. This folder represents the money you owe. When your cash flow is thin this folder gets fat. When you are flush with cash and decide to pay some vendors, find the oldest invoices you owe and pay them first. It is amazing how sloppily others keep their books, so do not rely on them to tell you how much you owe them. Keep track of it yourself this way.

When you pay an invoice, mark the date paid and check number on the stamp shown on plate 22 above and file it in Paid Invoices. If you make only a partial payment, mark it so and be sure to keep the invoice in Invoices Entered and Unpaid until it is paid in full.

Taxes. Whenever you get forms or letters in the mail from the IRS or the state in any way involving taxes, Social Security, withheld taxes, tax laws, or anything else which you want your accountant to see, stuff it in this folder. Remind him to check this folder each time he visits your office. If anything urgent comes in, don't wait. Call him right away. State and federal government agencies often make mistakes and send you demand notices for money you do not owe them. Your accountant will set them right in no uncertain terms. That's why you hire him.

Uncollected bills. This folder contains copies of bills you sent to your customers. When a customer makes a partial payment, mark it on the bill copy and replace the copy in the file. When the bill is paid up in full, move it to the proper **job** folder. If you follow this procedure perfectly, the total of accounts receivable in your books will equal the total of the amounts due in this folder. If not, some time at your leisure, track down the error and fix it.

You can survive with these few files but I am sure you will come up with plenty more. Enjoy.

CHAPTER 5

DISHONESTY AND HOW TO REACT TO IT

Dishonesty can ruin any personal or business relationship, so it must be watched for and eliminated without wasting any time. If you wait to address a dishonesty problem, you let it fester and get worse while you wait. The trouble with this advice is that sometimes it takes a while for you to be certain that dishonesty is happening. When you are certain, however, act promptly.

Dishonesty can attack from any source; your employee, your customer, your creditor, your partner, or even yourself. You need to be aware of your own motives and actions as well as those of others.

We once employed a painter who turned out to be dishonest on a spectacular scale. It began when he showed his co-workers a small textbook on how to get rich legally by going bankrupt. He had purchased the book for three dollars and said he was going to follow its advice. Well, he did. He borrowed a maximum size mortgage loan on his modest house. He applied for and received several major credit cards and borrowed up to the maximum on each without any security. He purchased a very expensive car and borrowed the maximum using the car as collateral. He then drove to a nearby foreign country and deposited all the borrowed cash in banks there, and returned home and filed for personal bankruptcy. At that time the bankruptcy law permitted a bankrupt person to keep both home and car, so his life did not change at all except that he now had a terrific car and a large nest egg of cash which he did not have before. When this scam was complete he offered to sell the little textbook to anyone who wanted it. Asking price; three dollars.

On the premise that he would defraud us as soon as he would defraud others, we found a legal way to get rid of him and did it quickly. (An interesting footnote to this saga; in the summer of 1998 someone he knew entered the trailer he was living in and murdered him.)

Partnerships are fragile. Members must always be available to their partners for consultation at any time and this is easy now that cellular telephones have become ubiquitous and cheap. If one employee or partner cannot be located for two hours on a given day it is not cause for concern but if the same thing happens every day it is a problem because that person is hiding something. People do not hide what they are proud of. They hide what they are ashamed of.

One of the greatest difficulties faced in any human relationship is gathering enough courage to tell someone important to you that something he is doing is bothering you. If you do not say it, it renders you angry. Your anger then becomes public whether or not you wish it to. If your employee, customer, or business partner is crabby in your presence, ASK IF SOMETHING YOU ARE DOING IS THE CAUSE. This will force the issue into the open and lead to discussion and solution. It may not force it open on the first try but it will eventually, so don't give up.

Bribery and extortion are another form of dishonesty, which will sometimes confront you as a contractor. I once had the painting contract on a large high rise apartment building, which was under construction. The clerk of the works (the owner's full time observer of the work of all the trades) had had no conversations with me at all, even though I was fully aware of his presence. The clerk has it in his power to make things very difficult for any contractor or subcontractor and because of that power he is in position to extort bribes if he chooses to. This clerk had found no fault with our work early in the job and I gave him no particular notice. Then, one day, the general contractor's construction superintendent said to me that the clerk wanted some paint to use repainting his house and implied that I should provide it free of charge. When I balked, the superintendent, who was at best a semi-honest guy, said, "What's two hundred dollars worth of paint on a $50,000 job? You want the job to run smooth, don't you?" I took a few days to think it over and decided to accede to the demand because $200 is not much money in such a large job. In other words, I rationalized dishonesty in the name of profit. I bought the paint, and without ever speaking directly to the clerk about it, left it on the floor in his job office.

About a month after the job was complete, the clerk showed up at my office and plunked down the paint I had given him. He apologized and said he was ashamed of his behavior and could not accept the bribe that he had previously accepted. That turnabout changed my attitude toward corruption. I vowed never again to succumb to extortion but then I had to figure out a way to avoid it. The technique I chose for avoiding it was simple but it always worked because a bribe-seeker hates to be explicit. He drops hints. You will never get a signed, registered letter asking for a bribe. My reaction to the hints is to laugh at them as though I am enjoying his joke. That places him in the position of either explicitly demanding the bribe (which he fears to do) or dropping it entirely, implying that it really was just a joke. In other words, the extortionist needs your cooperation in his crime and if you do not cooperate he is left adrift and cannot pull it off. I also believe that he is then afraid to harass you on the job, which is the threat originally implied for outright refusal to bribe, because it might lead you to expose him. Try this. It should work.

Dishonest treatment of you by your customers is a serious problem. In the long run you can avoid it by doing jobs only for trustworthy people but in the short run that avoidance is often impractical. If you are desperate for work and a new, unknown customer offers you a contract, you are most likely going to take it. That means you risk your money on his honesty, as well as his fiscal condition. Many people who are perfectly able to pay you will not pay you because they are dishonest.

Forcing debtors to pay what they owe is difficult and frustrating. Hiring a lawyer or a collection agency to chase for your money sometimes works and sometimes does not. In either case, if it does work, you still lose a substantial portion of the debt to pay for collection. Do not put a collection agency on retainer by paying in advance for its service whenever it is needed. Treat every collection problem on its own merits and decide how to proceed then. Some lawyers are very good at collections. I think it is a matter of personality. Ask around and find out which lawyers in your area have a reputation as effective collectors and use them. With some of them you may have to hold your nose but just remember how badly your customer is using you and lawyer may not smell so bad.

Do not let debtors get overdue on their bills without letting them know. If you do not let them know, they will assume that you have not noticed or that you do not care. If you do talk to them they are aware of your interest and cannot ignore you. A common ploy is for the customer to avoid you. "He is away from his desk." "He is in a meeting and will call you back as soon as it's over." "He's on the road and cannot be reached." "He's gone for the day but I told him that you are anxious to talk to him so I'm sure he'll call you first thing tomorrow."

If you get any or all of these avoidance clichés and you are not yet finished doing the job for this customer, STOP WORK. Do not complete the job under any circumstances until he pays you. Nothing grabs a cheater's attention as well as this perfectly legitimate pressure. It is even a good idea to clear out your equipment and materials so that he cannot use them to finish your work. This may not necessarily result in an immediate payment every time but it works in the long run. If your customer is trying to defraud you he will say almost anything to delay a showdown over the debt. "The check is in the mail." "Your check is all written and ready to mail but there is nobody here to sign it." "We lost your invoice." You will hear all of these excuses and a hundred more, many of which will be paragons of creativity. Just be relentless in your approach to collection and you will do as well as can be expected.

If your supplier or subcontractor fails to deliver material or labor as agreed, at least you are holding the money and that puts you in the driver's seat in any dispute resolution you might have with one of them. Do not, however, use that financial position to defraud them, because, if you do they will get even sooner or later. In fact, they may damage you with such finesse and subtlety that you never even know it happened. If your name becomes mud, your business will not last long.

CHAPTER 6

COST ESTIMATING
·····································

Most of the jobs you will be offered will be fixed price contracts based on pre-established specifications. In the case of buildings that do not yet exist, they will also be based on what is described in architectural plans. Since you are obligated to do the work for a fixed price, it would be wise for you to have an accurate idea of what the job will cost you to perform. As you may have guessed, this is the function called cost estimating.

Cost estimates are done for almost all jobs and their importance to your business cannot be overstated. Each estimate is comprised of the following parts;

1. Decision to bid. Sometimes it is wise not to bid a particular job. Each estimate costs money to do and some estimates are wasted because they never will lead to any work. You will have to make this decision based on your own experience with the people who ask you to bid. For example, two separate attitudes exist in the minds of general contractors concerning from whom to solicit subcontract bids. One approach is to solicit bids from every subcontractor, dead or alive, within two hundred miles and always take the lowest bid in every trade. This scattershot approach usually appeals to GCs who bid on public work, where the low bidder invariably gets the job. These contractors are usually big firms with lots of estimators and clerks who can do the work of gathering and summarizing vast amounts of bid information. Their approach is to use the low bidder in each trade, qualified or not, and then harass the hell out of the subcontractor and WITHHOLD PAYMENT for every real or imagined failure on the subcontractor's part to live up to the contract. A painter who knows his costs, manages well, and does his estimates carefully will never work for these scattershot GCs because he will never be the low bidder. The fools and the charlatans of the trade will always underbid him, so don't even try for scattershot work unless you are desperate and have nothing else.

The opposite attitude toward solicitation of subcontract bids is demonstrated by general contractors who work mostly for private property owners. Their bids to the owners have to be competitive in price but not necessarily lowest in order to get jobs. They nurture their reputations for quality, dispatch, experience, honest dealing, and so on, because their reputations get them work. They want subcontractors who will provide cooperation, quality, dispatch, and competitive prices. When I say competitive, I mean competitive with other quality subcontractors, not with fools and charlatans. These GCs will limit their requests for subcontract bids to a few good subs in each trade and will not accept bids from fools and charlatans. It is good to be on the list of repeat invitees of quality general contractors. Seek that status. It is obviously statistically easier to win a bidding competition against three other painters than against twenty. Jobs which are unwise to bid are also found in the repainting field. In Massachusetts, I have noticed, that all hotels, except for the very highest grade, seek bids based on price alone. As a result, their paint jobs are shockingly bad but they do not seem to care. It was fruitless therefore, for me to bother quoting to hotel managers. This, of course, may not be the case everywhere. *I now notice in 2016 that a new attitude seems to be coming into evidence. Hotels are now more often worth bidding for. I don't know why. Anyway, if you get a request from a hotel for a quotation, take a look at the quality level of its previous painting work and try to get a mental picture of what the hotel really wants (cheap and lousy or something better).*

2. Quantity survey. This is the first step in the actual process of estimating cost. It is the measurement of quantity of each of the various substrates needing your work. Most substrates are measured in units of area (commonly square feet), such as brick walls. Some are measured in linear feet, such as handrails, and some in individual units, such as door jambs. Your quantity survey is very simple in small jobs but can be very lengthy in large jobs. Therefore the clear organization of the estimate is extremely important. A useful format for the quantity survey is shown on plates 7 and 8 (estimating work sheet). Plate 7 shows it used to measure and list an interior job , and plate 8 an exterior job.

PLATE 7

PAGE 1 OF 1 JOB Simpson

| | | | | | | | | | SUBSTRATE | | | | |
AREA	L	W	H	OUTS	WALL	TRIM	CL'G	FLOOR	GWB ptd	conc. Floor	oak trim	door refin.	jamb ptd.
lobby	20	20	9		x	x			720				
men	8	10	8 4' dado		x	x			144+80	80			
auditorium	32	44	10		x		x	x	1520		80	8	6
all													
TOTALS									2464	80	80	8	6

76

PLATE 8

	A	B	C	D	E	F	G	H	I	K	L	M	N	O	P
1				PAGE		1 OF		1 JOB	Arcon Plastics						
3												SUBSTRATE			
5	AREA	L	W	H		OUTS	WALL	TRIM	CL'G FLOOR	brick pt'd	CB pt'd	window	jamb	rib deck	
7	north	100		25	150sf	x				2350		20			
8	east	50		25	50sf	x		x			1200	7	1	200	
9	south	100		25		x				2500		15			
10	west	50		25		x				1250		7	2		
11															
43				TOTALS						6100	1200	49	3	200	

Notice on plate 7 that the walls, ceilings, and floors are measured in square feet and the oak baseboard in linear feet. Also notice that no outs were taken for doors and windows. This is a standard procedure in estimating painting (but not in measuring for wall covering, though. I assume that you measure wall covering in strips of various lengths. This form is equally useful for that approach). In the room labeled "men", there is a ceramic tile dado 48" high. You should take out that surface, as did this imaginary estimator. Also notice on plate 8 that when you measure *exterior* walls, you record only two dimensions, length and height. I always use this form on a sheet of paper 8.5"x18" so as to get as many columns and lines in use as possible. Some estimates require the use of all the columns, even on an 18" long form.

Standards of measurement vary from estimator to estimator. For example, some measure the size of a door jamb and carry the figure in linear feet. Others, including me, prefer to call a jamb a jamb and keep records on how much labor and material are required to do one. Then when we find unusual jambs which are more time consuming to paint than a standard jamb, we use multiples. Another example; a single hollow metal frame is one jamb. A wider one with two doors hung in it is still one jamb because it requires the same labor to paint it (doors are listed separately). A combined jamb and single sidelight is considered two jambs, because it takes about twice as long to paint as a single jamb. Your experience may tell you otherwise and you may decide to call a jamb and sidelight 1.8 times a jamb instead of the 2 times that I have suggested. If you do, don't let me try to talk you out of it. Your cost experience is very important to your viability as a businessperson. Keep your own unit cost records as a matter of course. Unit cost means simply the cost to do one unit, such as the square foot, linear foot or door jamb. Unit cost record keeping will be explained in detail in chapter seven.

If you decide to limit your work to jobs small enough to estimate by the man-hour or man-day, then let me admonish you to do your estimates equally as carefully as you would if you were using the unit cost approach. Let us imagine that you are called upon to give a quote on repainting the inside of a large, ornate house. Most rooms call for new wallpaper as well as repainting all woodwork and plaster ceilings. Using the estimate work sheet, list all the rooms in the left column. Then title the substrate columns as mask; wash-patch plaster; woodwork; doors; windows; radiators; wallpaper prep; wallpaper hang; and so on. Then just enter the number of man-hours or man-days you expect to spend on each item in the lines below for each room. This seemingly fussy work prevents you from forgetting any item and it gives you a written record to compare with your actual labor usage when you do the job. This is important because it makes your estimates more and more accurate as the years go by.

Except for wallpaper, the cost of material on this type of job is negligible enough to just guess at in a lump sum on the recap sheet, so you could choose not to enter material on the work sheet.

Each column will then be totaled at the bottom of the work sheet in hours. Your estimate recap sheet (plate 13)

PLATE 13

JOB   *27 Ripon Street*   BID DUE DATE   *4/16/04*

ARCHITECT   PHONE

OWNER   *John Somers*   SECTION   ADDENDA

POSTED PAY SCALE   COST PER HOUR   *30.00*

HOURS	PROCESS	QUAN	LUC	MUC	EXT
733	*LABOR*	*733 HRS*	*26.00*		*21,990*
	MATERIALS, PAINT, ETC.				*450*
30	*CONTINGENCIES*	*30 HR*	*S 26.00*		*900*
	WALLPAPER (SUPPLIED BY OWNER)				
	TOTALS				*23,340*

PROFIT   *2,300*

PRICE   *26,640*

then becomes very simple, with a line for labor, a line for materials, a line for wallpaper, a line for contingencies, and a line for setup and clean out. Look at plate 13 now for an example. *Oops, I just noticed in 2016 that I goofed when designing PLATE 13. I forget to enter the estimated labor hours for set up and clean out. Every job estimate needs this entry on the recap sheet (plate 10).*

This estimate recap form (return to plate 10 now) is the form on which dollar values are calculated and summed up. This is also the most difficult part of any estimate because it requires you to make comparisons of the expected unit costs with your previous unit costs on similar jobs you have done. You do that by referring to your unit cost records as shown in plates 4, 5, and 6

PLATE 4

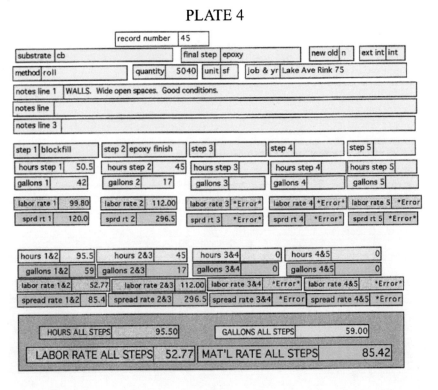

	record number	45

| substrate | cb | | final step | epoxy | | new old | n | ext int | int |

| method | roll | | quantity | 5040 | unit | sf | job & yr | Lake Ave Rink 75 |

notes line 1	WALLS. Wide open spaces. Good conditions.
notes line	
notes line 3	

step 1	blockfill	step 2	epoxy finish	step 3		step 4		step 5	
hours step 1	50.5	hours step 2	45	hours step 3		hours step 4		hours step 5	
gallons 1	42	gallons 2	17	gallons 3		gallons 4		gallons 5	
labor rate 1	99.80	labor rate 2	112.00	labor rate 3	*Error*	labor rate 4	*Error*	labor rate 5	*Error*
sprd rt 1	120.0	sprd rt 2	296.5	sprd rt 3	*Error*	sprd rt 4	*Error*	sprd rt 5	*Error*

hours 1&2	95.5	hours 2&3	45	hours 3&4	0	hours 4&5	0
gallons 1&2	59	gallons 2&3	17	gallons 3&4	0	gallons 4&5	0
labor rate 1&2	52.77	labor rate 2&3	112.00	labor rate 3&4	*Error*	labor rate 4&5	*Error*
spread rate 1&2	85.4	spread rate 2&3	296.5	spread rate 3&4	*Error	spread rate 4&5	*Error

HOURS ALL STEPS	95.50	GALLONS ALL STEPS	59.00
LABOR RATE ALL STEPS	52.77	MAT'L RATE ALL STEPS	85.42

PLATE 5

record number	13

substrate	balustrade		final step	varnish		new old	n	ext int	int

method	brush		quantity	68	unit	lf	job & yr	Quabog Rubber 80

notes line 1: Hardwood balustrade on 2' high hardwood balcony edge (included) all of which was stained,

notes line: sealed TWICE, and varnished. Spindles were 4" on center.

notes line 3: First class job.

step 1	all steps	step 2		step 3		step 4		step 5	
hours step 1	43	hours step 2		hours step 3		hours step 4		hours step 5	
gallons 1		gallons 2		gallons 3		gallons 4		gallons 5	
labor rate 1	1.58	labor rate 2	*Error*	labor rate 3	*Error*	labor rate 4	*Error*	labor rate 5	*Error
sprd rt 1	*Error*	sprd rt 2	*Error*	sprd rt 3	*Error*	sprd rt 4	*Error*	sprd rt 5	*Error*

hours 1&2	43	hours 2&3	0	hours 3&4	0	hours 4&5	0
gallons 1&2	0	gallons 2&3	0	gallons 3&4	0	gallons 4&5	0
labor rate 1&2	1.58	labor rate 2&3	*Error*	labor rate 3&4	*Error*	labor rate 4&5	*Error*
spread rate 1&2	###	spread rate 2&3	*Error*	spread rate 3&4	*Error*	spread rate 4&5	*Error

HOURS ALL STEPS	43.00	GALLONS ALL STEPS	0.00
LABOR RATE ALL STEPS	1.58	MAT'L RATE ALL STEPS	*Error*

PLATE 6

record number	336

substrate	sm surf		final step	paint		new old	o	ext int	int

method	spray		quantity	16000	unit	sf	job & yr	Mary Chapel, HC 82

notes line 1: WALLS AND CEILINGS together in vaulted chapel. Pews, floors, statues, fixtures

notes line: masked first. Major masking job. It cost $626 for masking materials. Plaster patching

notes line 3: was major enough to subcontract, therefore not included here.

step 1	Mask & cover.	step 2	wash	step 3	prime	step 4	intermediate	step 5	finish
hours step 1	101.5	hours step 2	16.5	hours step 3	30	hours step 4	29	hours step 5	29
gallons 1		gallons 2		gallons 3	50	gallons 4	60	gallons 5	60
labor rate 1	157.64	labor rate 2	969.70	labor rate 3	533.33	labor rate 4	551.72	labor rate 5	551.72
sprd rt 1	*Error*	sprd rt 2	*Error*	sprd rt 3	320.0	sprd rt 4	266.67	sprd rt 5	266.7

hours 1&2	118	hours 2&3	46.5	hours 3&4	59	hours 4&5	58
gallons 1&2	0	gallons 2&3	50	gallons 3&4	110	gallons 4&5	120
labor rate 1&2	135.59	labor rate 2&3	344.09	labor rate 3&4	271.19	labor rate 4&5	275.86
spread rate 1&2	###	spread rate 2&3	320.0	spread rate 3&4	145.5	spread rate 4&5	133.3

HOURS ALL STEPS	206.00	GALLONS ALL STEPS	170.00
LABOR RATE ALL STEPS	77.67	MAT'L RATE ALL STEPS	94.12

or other people's unit cost records, such as those of the PDCA. Chapter 8 contains information about PDCA (Painting and Decorating Contractors of America).

The heading section is important to you as reference information. Many times you will do an estimate and hear nothing about the job for a year, then suddenly get a contract in the mail. By that time, of course, you will have forgotten all the details. All you need to do, though, is to dig out the estimate and it will all come back to you. Section number means the part of the specifications you are bidding on. If an architect is involved, he will not only draw plans but will write specifications detailing what he wants each trade to do. Usually section 09900 describes the work done by painters. You may wish to bid more than one section. If you do, list them all on the form header. Addenda are changes made by the designer after plans and specifications are distributed to bidders. Read them to see if they affect your price and list on the form header which ones you have seen and are including in your bid. In the case of this hypothetical job, there is a posted rate because it is a public building being worked on. The pay scale for painters is set at $20.07 per hour. You must pay this rate even though it may exceed what you ordinarily pay your painters. Therefore you have to calculate what you expect your total hourly cost will be when you add to the wages the overhead costs (Chapter 11 will explain how to do that). So, fill in that figure on the form header as a reminder of what cost you expect for each hour worked.

The lines below the header reuse all the quantity information from the estimating work sheet (plates 7 and 8). The column on the left edge of the estimating recap is very important because it shows man-hours needed to perform the work. Notice that the first line carries 3,290 square feet of masonry walls. The estimator figures that the labor will cost $.51 per square foot at an hourly labor cost of $40 and the material will cost $.21 per square foot for a total cost of $.72. (LUC means labor unit cost, MUC, material unit cost, and TUC, total unit cost). Multiplying the TUC by the quantity (3290x.72) produces $2,368.80. Round that off to the nearest dollar and you get $2,369. Now you translate that line into man-hours needed to do that job of block filler and two coats of epoxy.

To reach man-hours you multiply quantity by LUC and divide the answer by the $40 cost per man hour previously determined (3290x.51/40). The quotient of that calculation is 41.94. Again, round off to the nearest hour and you get 42 hours as the time you expect to spend on that particular process. If your usual cost per man-hour is $28.00, then you would, of course, divide the LUC by 28. In this case, using $28 per hour, the LUC would be $.36 and the hours would still be 42. If this sounds arcane, do not worry. Chapter 7 will explain how you know what the labor unit cost (LUC) will be.

The next two lines, jambs and doors, are recorded by the piece, not by the square foot. Jambs can be done, according to this estimator, in 45 minutes each, and doors in one hour each.

The next three lines on this estimate are all items which can be listed by hours in the quantity column. The backstops are a miscellaneous item which must be done as part of the job but do not lend themselves to costing by ordinary means. How many basketball backstops do you paint each week ?

The last two items, I suggest, belong on every estimate. Contingencies can be defined as "things that go wrong". It is a rare job that runs perfectly smoothly from beginning to end, and your unit cost records, which we will examine in chapter 7, do not include contingencies. Set up and clean up time at the start and finish of a job are not included in unit cost records, either, so they must be added. Your own knowledge of the customer, job location, equipment needed, and so forth will serve to tell you how many hours to apply to these last two items. For example, you estimate that the actual working time for a job should be 300 hours but you know the customer is a seriously disorganized general contractor who cannot coordinate the work of his subcontractors well. For him, add a little extra contingency time.

The bottom of the estimating recap form is where you come up with the price. Remember that, so far, you have only considered cost. Now you add on the profit you hope to make. Your decision on profit depends on all the variables about competition, general business conditions, how hungry you are etc. Only you can make the decision. So, do it carefully and good luck !

The notes space reminds the estimator to notify the person who actually bids the job (usually the boss) of any information pertinent to the bid. In this case, he reminds the boss that the work will be done in the company's busiest month. The conditions space tells the boss that we did not include a specific item which may have been included in section 09900 but which we do not wish to do. It tells the boss not to forget to qualify the bid by adding the condition that you are excluding such and such from your bid.

When a painting job is complete, it is fascinating to compare the estimated hours from this estimating recap with the actual hours spent (from the job cost sheet described in chapter 4). This little exercise tells you how accurate your estimates are.

When you get sophisticated enough to have a computerized recap sheet for your estimates, there is an improvement over the hand written one shown above. With your computer doing the calculating and addition, you can speed up your work and reduce arithmetic errors. See plate 23 for a sample.

PLATE 23

JOB   BID DUE DATE

ARCHITECT   PHONE

OWNER   SECTION   ADDENDA

POSTED PAY SCALE   COST PER HOUR *$26.00*

HRS	SUBSTRATE	PROCESS	QUAN	U	LPR	MSR	MC/G	LUC	MUC	TUC	EXT
13.4	conc block	2 coats flat latex rolled	2340	sf	175	200	14.50	0.149	0.072	0.221	517
12.0	hm jambs, new	2 coats enamel brushed	16	ea	1.33	9	24.00	19.549	2.667	22.216	355
16.0	flush wood drs	stain, seal, and 2 varnish	16	ea	1	7	20.00	26.000	2.857	28.857	462
48.8	smooth plaster	2 coats latex flat rolled	10986	sf	225	190	14.50	0.115	0.076	0.192	2106
12.0		staging & contingencies	12	hrs	1			26.000		26.000	312
102		TOTALS									3754

The header and footer information are unchanged from the earlier version, so ignore them and direct your attention to the top line.

This line uses codes, so read across with me and I will describe their uses. The first column (HRS) is man-hours. The number on each line in this column is automatically calculated by the computer from two lines further to the right, namely QUAN and LPR. QUAN means quantity of units and LPR means labor productivity rate. The computer divides the QUAN (which in this case on line one is 2,340 square feet) by

175 (the number of units of quantity you expect a painter to perform in one hour).

Now go back to the column headers and look at the second column.

Its title is SUBSTRATE (the surface or item to be worked on). On line one this example says "conc block" which is the code for concrete blocks. The QUAN is 2340 and the U (unit) is "sf" (square feet).

PROCESS means what you do to the substrate and you all ready know that QUAN means quantity and U means unit. The next two columns do not appear in the simplified hand written recap shown previously. They are LPR (labor productivity rate) and MSR (material spreading rate). When you price a job, you estimate both of these rates from your past experience and your unit cost records. When using the simple hand written recap you have to manually translate these rates into dollar figures for the labor and material unit costs. However, with this computerized recap format, you need only fill in the rates and the computer does everything else, with one slight caveat. That is, you have to enter a material cost per gallon of whatever material you will use for the particular process. In line one, column MC/G, I have entered $14.50 as the cost for one gallon of paint. The computer then knows all it needs to know for it to calculate values to enter in LUC, MUC, TUC, and EXT (Extension). Extension is the product of the quantity times the total unit cost.

Now look at line two. It describes 16 hollow metal jambs to be painted by hand two coats. Past experience tells you that you can do 1.33 of them per hour and that one gallon of paint will cover 9 of them. Enamel costs $24.00 per gallon.

As soon as you have entered this much information, all the other spaces fill in automatically along that line.

Now direct your attention to the bottom line of the recap sheet. You will notice that the computer has added up the total of man-hours needed and the total estimated cost in dollars.

Sometime, when you are ready for it, I recommend this type of spread sheet as an estimating time saver, but don't hurry. It will wait while you work out all the big bugs in your business first.

CHAPTER 7

UNIT COSTS AND HOW TO

RECORD AND USE THEM
....

The unit cost is the cost in labor and material to paint one unit of measure. The most common unit of measure is the square foot and the most common unit cost used by painting contractors is the cost per square foot . If it costs $.27 to perform one painting process on one square foot of surface and you know it, you can easily estimate the cost for all the square feet of the same surface needing work by simple multiplication.

Before starting any job you have to deliver your equipment, tools, and materials. Upon completion you have to remove them from the premises. This is true of any job, regardless of size. If you have to spray an acoustic tile ceiling which is fifteen feet above the floor, it does not matter whether you have 1000 square feet or 50,000 square feet to spray. The cost of painting each square foot is the same and the cost of setting up the job is the same in either case. For that reason, I strongly recommend that your unit cost records do not include set up time (see the previous chapter on estimating recapitulation, if you have forgotten how to do this). Unit cost records need to be kept unpolluted by extraneous information like setup time. The PDCA (Painting and Decorating Contractors of America) publishes unit cost records each year for its members. Its format is simple.

It excludes preparation of surfaces and displays LUC (labor unit cost) in units per hour and MUC (material unit cost) in units per gallon for actual painting only. It wisely refrains from publishing dollar costs per square foot because labor costs per hour constantly change and paint costs per gallon do likewise. Therefore, the contractor referring to PDCA unit costs has to translate productivity rates per hour and spreading rates per gallon into dollar costs per unit (usually, per square foot). Since the PDCA excludes preparation from its unit cost records, the value of those records is limited to painting only. If you use them, you need to add your own unit costs for preparatory work. As long as you are aware of this you will not get into trouble using them. (NOTE: Since I originally wrote this chapter, the PDCA has begun recording productivity for preparatory work also, which makes its information even more valuable to you than it was before).

Here is how you do it. First you establish your cost per hour for employing a painter. You can generally use the average cost per hour since presumably your painters are paid at differing wage scales relating to their skill, knowledge, and productivity. (If you pay them all the same rate of pay, then this decision does not have to be made.) Assuming a variety of wage rates in your shop, ranging from $18 down to $8 per hour, you will have previously calculated the total cost per hour for each rate on a form such as this.

WAGE	FIXED O/H	VAR O/H	HOURLY COST
18.00	7.00	9.00	34.00
17.00	7.00	8.50	32.50
16.00	7.00	8.00	31.00
15.00	7.00	7.50	29.50
14.00	7.00	7.00	28.00
13.00	7.00	6.50	26.50
12.00	7.00	6.00	25.00
11.00	7.00	5.50	23.50
10.00	7.00	5.00	22.00
9.00	7.00	4.50	20.50
8.00	7.00	4.00	19.00

The full, unabbreviated, titles for each column above are "hourly wage", "fixed overhead", "variable overhead", and "total hourly cost".

Let's assume that your average wage rate is $12.00 per hour, which gives you an average total cost per hour of $25.00. Remember, all of these numbers are purely hypothetical. Overhead costs vary greatly from state to state and from business to business. You will need to develop your own numbers from experience. Chapter 11 describes how this is done.

Just a word of caution; if you are bidding a job which requires ALL highly skilled people, don't use your average hourly cost on your estimating recap. Use a higher figure. An apprentice at $8 per hour can be used on block filling along with more experienced people but he is of no use and cannot be used on a marbleizing job.

Next, you go to the unit cost records which you are using, whether they are your own, PDCA's, or any other proprietary records, and look up what you can expect for productivity per hour for labor and spreading rate per gallon for paint. For example, let's say the substrate in question is previously painted concrete block, which requires no preparation. You will roll on one coat of latex flat paint in near perfect conditions. Your unit cost records say you can expect a painter to do 207 square feet per hour and the paint to cover 133 square feet per gallon. To get LUC (labor unit cost) you divide your cost per hour, in this case $25.00, by 207. This results in a LUC of $.12. To get material unit cost, divide the cost per gallon (let's call it $15.00) by the spreading rate of 133 square feet. This results in a MUC of $.11 and a TUC (total unit cost) of $.23 per square foot. You will notice that I rounded off the quotients (unit costs) to the nearest penny.

Now, you may ask, how do you know what your productivity and spreading rates are? This vitally important information is gathered painstakingly over the years and recorded. However, if you are a new business, you have none yet, but you still need something to go by. This is where you must rely on cost information gathered by others until you have gathered your own. Spreading rates are readily available from paint manufacturers' catalogues but labor rates are jealously kept secret by your competitors if they know them. More often than not, they do not know them and that gives you an advantage if you do. Also, there now exist some books which provide some useful unit costs. These can be found on the internet.

Here are some examples from the data base I have developed over decades. This information was originally kept in a computerized data base, specifically Microsoft Works. However, Microsoft no longer publishes Works and has replaced it with Excel which is a combination of database and spread sheet programs. Excel is wonderful for spread sheet work but not as good as its predecessor, Microsoft Works, for data base use work. No doubt there exist plenty of others you could use, possibly just as good. Your computerized database of unit cost records must be able to show up in either list form or data form. Please turn to plate 4 in the illustrations and follow along with my explanation. This first example is from a concrete block painting job. Starting at the top left, it lists the substrate, concrete blocks with the code "CB". Encoding, rather than writing out the whole substrate name, produces the advantage of your being able to lump several substrates together under one code. For example, I lump smooth plaster, gypsum drywall, and skim coat plaster under the single substrate code, "SM SURF", meaning smooth surface. The next field along the top line lists the final step (epoxy, in this case). This field is necessary for searching the data base. Other final steps could be, "paint, varnish, clear waterproof, sandblast" or any others that fit your needs. The data base program is very flexible, so it can accurately suit your business. The next field in the top line is new old. This actually was an existing building but it was in perfect condition as if new, so I listed it as new. The next field in the top line tells you whether it was indoor or outdoor work. On the second line the first field is method. You can surely see how important this field is. The next field is the one in which you enter the quantity done. In the case of this sample, the quantity is 5,040 and the unit of measure is square feet, which shows up in the next field, entitled "unit". Most substrates are measured in square feet in the painting industry, but not all. Some, such as baseboard or chair rail, are measured in linear feet, and some are measured by the piece, such as doors, and some are measured by the square inch, such as gilding. The field calling for the job name and year is not critical but I find it useful in recalling the conditions from memory. Of course, if your estimator never saw the job, that will not do any good and he will have to rely on the notes in the next three fields. The section for notes uses three lines in order to give you plenty of space to describe the conditions under which the job was done. You will find that the more information you put into notes, the more valuable the record will be.

Next you have a block of five columns representing five possible steps in any paint job. It is rare that all five are needed, but not impossible. In this case there were only two steps, block filling and epoxy finishing. You enter the number of man-hours spent on block filling (in this case, 50.5 hours). The computer then automatically calculates the labor productivity per hour by dividing 5,040 square feet by 50.5 hours. This produces the labor rate of 99.8 square feet per hour for block filling on this particular job.

Reading down the step #1 column, the material used in step one is entered (in this case, 42 gallons). Always use gallons or decimal portions of gallons. If you keep some records in quarts, liters, or barrels, you will get mixed up. The next field is automatically calculated by the computer as a spreading rate for the block filler of 120 square feet per gallon. It did this by dividing 5,040 square feet, (the quantity from line two) by 42 gallons.

Now you move right to step #2, epoxy finish. Here you enter 45 hours and 17 gallons and the computer calculates the rates as 296.5 square feet per gallon for material use, and 112 square feet per hour for labor. Notice that a symbol called "*Error" shows up in the rest of the spaces normally calculated by the computer. That merely shows that no information was entered for it to use. It means nothing to you.

The next two lines give you automatically calculated rates in groups of two steps. You may think this is weird, wacko, and a waste of time but it is not. It is not a waste of time because it takes no time. The computer does all the work from the information you previously typed in above and does it instantly. It is not even weird or wacko because you may well have to compare the total unit costs from two steps on one record with the same two steps from another record in which three or four steps were recorded. Also, sometimes when you are gathering man-hour records from a job, you may not be able to separate the time spent block filling from the time spent finishing with epoxy. Rather than discarding the information you can save it and use it in the future as one combined step. It is ALWAYS better to have some information than to have no information.

The final fields on this unit cost record appear in the big box at the bottom. These are the fields most frequently referred to. They show you labor and material rates for the whole process from start to finish.

The computer did all the work. All you have to do is reap the benefit.

Now let's go back up to the notes section of the form for a minute. The more information you put in here the better. It helps you or your estimator to better visualize the conditions of the job if you fill these lines carefully and completely. Furthermore, some painters' processes cannot be described in words alone in the NOTES fields. They need a sketch to describe the substrate. Look at plate one and you will see a sketch of what may look like a blob of chocolate melting in the sun.

PLATES 1 AND 2

CURVED SIDE STAINED AND VARNISHED

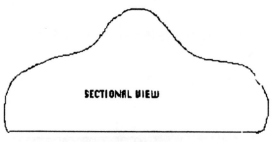

SECTIONAL VIEW

FLAT SIDE PAINTED

1	2	3
4	5	6
7	8	9

Plate 1 shows the cross section view of a piece of wood trim used as a false muntin in a window. It fits tightly against the glass with its flat side touching the glass. Its purpose is to mimic a real wood muntin dividing a window into lights of glass. Sometimes you have to stain one side and paint the other in order to have it look right. How else than by using a sketch, could you describe it in your unit cost records? Now look at plate 2. This shows a window sash divided up into lights of glass, shown here numbered. I decided years ago to record the unit cost on windows with small lights of glass by the light instead of by the entire window. It worked moderately well but not perfectly. If all windows were sliders, or all were double hung, or all were casements, perhaps that method of cost recording would work fine. However, they are not. Casement windows, for example, on the interior side, require more labor than double hung windows of the same number of lights.

This method or recording by lights works well, however, with removable or "snap-in" muntins as described above in plate 1. I call each space as shown numbered in plate 2 a "light". That makes for an easy way to record the work of finishing these things without having to do a lot of measuring.

Next, please turn to plate 5. This sample records the labor required to stain and varnish a wood balustrade and the edge of the balcony just below it in a new office building. It was recorded as one combined step only and material usage was not recorded, so it could have been a better record if done with more detail. Yet, it should be easy for you to see that it is very valuable information. Just for fun, to see a unit cost record which uses the fields for all five steps, see plate 6.

PLATE 6

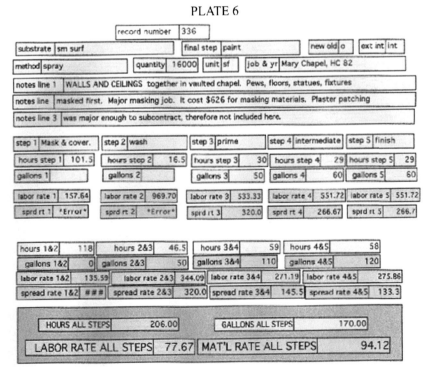

By now, you might have concluded, if you have waded through all this turgid stuff, that you might need to list the standards of measurement that your business uses so that each estimator will use the same standards. For example, if you measure fences by the square foot of face surface on both sides and your partner measures them by linear feet, your estimator measures them by square feet on one side, and your mother-in-law measures them by the ton of trash the wind blows against them, your business could have a headache. So, be sure to codify the standards of measurements you want all of you to use.

CHAPTER 8

SOURCES OF USEFUL INFORMATION

Information and the use of it is what separates the sheep from the goats in any business. Whenever you find any information that is useful, use it. If you cannot use it now, save it to use later. This may sound elementary but it is not easy to do unless you are organized. Obviously, a computerized data base with multiple cross references etc, is the best organization but you have more urgent things to do when you are getting your business started. So, I suggest this simple method to use at first. Keep a file drawer in which you will store all possibly useful stuff that comes through the mail.

Organize it by;

1. price lists for tools and equipment from suppliers

2. brochures describing rental equipment

3. technical journal articles which tell how to perform unusual tasks which you rarely need to do.

4. color samples from all paint manufacturers

5. product catalogs from all paint manufacturers

6. names and addresses of all sources of useful information

7. And so on and so on. You get the idea.

You will not open this drawer in search of knowledge very often but when you do, you will strain a muscle patting yourself on the back.

I once had the task assigned to me by my successors in business (after I retired from management) to devise a technique for applying a real sand finish to the exterior of an antique building. The building is a theater which was built before the Civil War in the Greek Revival style of architecture. The facade was made of cast iron, wood, and sheet metal but it was supposed to look as though it were built of stone, like the Parthenon. The method in common use in the 18th and early 19th centuries was to stick sand to all the various substrates so that they all looked like sandstone. We had to restore this sand texture and my task was to figure out how to do it. Well, luck was with me. The day I began experimenting on the problem, I took time out to read a trade journal which came that day in the mail. In it was an article describing the very process I was trying to invent and how to do it. Was that good luck or what ? The moral to this story is, READ THE TRADE JOURNALS and SAVE THEM. (Another moral is to always have good luck).

Business, trade, and professional organizations are a great source of useful information. The PDCA (Painting and Decorating Contractors of America) is a must for you to join. It has active local chapters nearly everywhere. These locals meet regularly and address themselves to issues affecting their business. The national organization produces a monthly journal full of valuable articles and ads. Furthermore the national also schedules education and training classes for contractors all over the country. I can attest from personal experience that it does a very good job.

If you work for and with architects, engineers, and general contractors on a regular basis, then the CSI (Construction Specifications Institute) is a good choice for you to join. Its professional journal is not painting-specific, as is the PDCA's, so it is less valuable to you, but the local chapter meetings can well be more valuable than PDCA because of the contacts you make. For many years, our business was the only painting contractor in the local chapter and that gave us a valuable edge over the competition in the field of knowing the architects and what they had on their drawing boards. All I had to do was attend CSI meetings and not make a fool of myself.

The chamber of commerce is valuable in that its members know the names of other members and send business their way at times. A membership in that local organization could be useful depending upon what type of work you choose to do. You can decide that based on your knowledge of your local area.

If you go heavily into sand blasting and industrial work, a membership in the SSPC (Structural Steel Painting Council) is a must. It is another national organization with an excellent trade journal full of fascinating articles on maintenance coatings.

Some publishers produce trade journals about painting. These often come to you by mail without your having ordered them. The publisher makes his money by selling advertising, so he does not care much about subscription fees. A large circulation is what sells ads. These magazines can be very useful because they introduce you to new and improved tools, equipment, and products which you might not know about otherwise.

Product catalogues from major paint manufacturers are obviously designed to sell products but for you they can be an invaluable source of knowledge on what primers to use on what substrates under what finishes.

The companies which specialize in making maintenance coatings do the best job of educating the painter and the coatings engineer. Get and keep as many of these catalogues as you can.

Finally, you must keep unit cost records from your own jobs. Develop the habit of doing so and your bidding will become more and more accurate as time goes on. See plates 4 through 6 for my suggested format. It should be computerized for easy searching. You should start out with a purchased open ended unit cost data base and keep adding to it. Such information is available via the internet.

CHAPTER 9

ADVERTISING
....

Some advertising is necessary for any business but the trick is not to waste money on advertising which brings in no business, or worse, which brings in the kind of business you don't want. So, before deciding on where to advertise, you must first have decided what sort of work you wish to attract. Let me refer you back to chapter 2, KNOWING YOUR CUSTOMERS. Let's look at advertising which might work for each of the eight different types of customers described in that chapter.

THE MERCHANT, because of his rare need for a painter, and his desire to keep down cost, is a tough bird to attract. He will certainly be interested in your ability to provide his needed service, but that ability cannot really be shown in advertising. If your ad says a lot of complimentary things about you, his response will be "ho-hum" because everybody else's ads will do the same. You might as well just use the phrase "commercial work" in your ad and rely on that to attract the merchant's business. When a merchant responds to your ad, it is then up to you to sell him on your ability to respond to his needs. The ad is merely your foot in the door. For the merchant, my recommendation is YELLOW PAGES.

THE SHORT TERM REAL ESTATE DEVELOPER. In my opinion there is no medium of advertising which will reach these people. If you want their business you must go to them directly and sell yourself. Forget about speculative builders of new houses. It is impossible to get their business at prices high enough to cover your costs.

Developers of <u>commercial</u> real estate can, and sometimes are, a good source of business for painting contractors. They do not, however, read ads in yellow pages, trade magazines, or newspaper classified ads when looking for subcontractors. They ask around. If you are new in business, their asking around will not help you because nobody knows you. Therefore, advertising will do you no good to get their business. You must go to them and sell yourself. Joining organizations where you will come into contact with them makes it easier by breaking the ice. My recommendation for short term real estate developers is NO ADVERTISING.

THE LONG TERM REAL ESTATE DEVELOPER/MANAGER. This guy can be your meal ticket but it isn't easy to sell him. He also asks around if he is seeking new contractors. He asks other real estate managers, architects, and general contractors. Sometimes he even asks contractors in other trades. He does not read yellow pages or newspaper classified ads because he does not believe all the hype the ads are loaded with. So, your best source of this type of business is the relations you have with general contractors, other subs, and architects. Your best immediate way to get to know them is to join organizations where you will mix with them. Your best long range way to get them on your side is to work with them, do a good job, cooperate fully and gain their respect.

I recommend NO ADVERTISING other than word of mouth.

INSTITUTIONS usually fall into the same category as LONG TERM REAL ESTATE MANAGEMENT in that they are unapproachable until you have a solid reputation. That reputation is developed through the same sources as described above. However, some colleges, especially those with big maintenance budgets, will have so many painting jobs to award each year that they put them out to competitive bidding with less than usual background knowledge of their bidders. These can be approached simply by walking in and requesting them to invite you to bid. They will be wary of you at first and only take bids from you on small jobs with flexible time requirements. But after you establish a reputation with them they will start inviting your bids on all jobs. I recommend NO ADVERTISING other than word of mouth.

HOMEOWNERS will definitely look you up in the Yellow Pages. Your ad there must say that you do residential work, and must not mention price. If it does mention price, you will waste tons of time trying unsuccessfully to compete with off-duty firefighters, college students on vacation, and anybody else who knows how to dip a brush into a liquid and spread that liquid on a board. I recommend YELLOW PAGES.

CORROSION ENGINEERS, when employed in private industry, might well look for you in the yellow pages. If you want their business you should use a phrase in your ad such as "industrial coatings" or "corrosion prevention coatings". If the yellow pages in your area have listings for such specialties, advertise in them as well as under painting. I have found that several distinct listings under different categories of business service, while inexpensive, are often productive. If you do this type of work you will also probably do sand blasting. If so, list your name and telephone number under that category also. Corrosion engineers working for a government agency will not look for you anywhere because they advertise for bids on public work in the open marketplace. They don't find you. You find them. So, for private corrosion engineers, I recommend YELLOW PAGES.

DECORATORS. Ah, decorators. They make their mark and make their money selling materials first and services second. Therefore, they are to be found in the company of people who deal in furniture, wall covering, paint, carpets, plumbing fixtures, fine arts, and everything else that affects interior ambience. In order to court them, you must court all their friends and acquaintances too. Leave your business card and the memory of your smile at each of those places of business where decorators might turn up, and keep on leaving them. For the sake of direct contact after you have gotten their attention, all you need is a place where they can look up your number. I recommend YELLOW PAGES.

BUREAUCRATS. You don't advertise for them. They advertise for you.

The only medium I have recommended so far is yellow pages. But others exist and should be discussed here. For example, signs. If you have company vehicles they make for an excellent and very cheap form of ads because they are always traveling around exposing your name and logo all over town. Get a good commercial artist to design a logo for you, make sure that you like it, and never change it. Constant repetitive exposure burns your logo into the public's mind and becomes a familiar background item, and familiarity breeds trust. A potential customer who is subconsciously familiar with your name will be favorably disposed to you in advance without realizing it.

Radio and television advertising should be zealously avoided. Radio ads scatter the message helter skelter to hundreds or thousands of people at random who will never remember your ad when they need painting work unless you have repeated it so many times that they puke upon hearing it yet again. Do the listening public and yourself a favor.

Don't advertise on radio. Television is also scattershot, even more so than radio. It is simply not equipped to address a specific market. Whenever I see a restaurant advertising on television, I immediately make a solemn vow never to eat there. My reasoning is that, if they are so desperate to get customers in their doors, their food must be truly awful. And, if they have to cover the cost of television advertising in the price of each meal, they must also charge too much. Do not advertise on TV. Potential customers could well be unfavorably disposed toward you if you do.

In my experience, classified advertising in daily newspapers only attracts customers looking for a sucker contractor to do the work below cost because he is ignorant of what his costs are or because he is ignorant of what pricing the market will bear. Weekly newspapers serving a specific market which you may wish to penetrate may be a better idea because the rates are cheap and the readers homogeneous. For example, everywhere in the USA it seems, real estate people are printing weekly ads for houses interspersed with filler "news" articles designed to enhance real estate sales. These flyers, usually sent free to "occupant", concentrate on the housing market, so if that is what you want, go for it.

CHAPTER 10

INSURANCE
....

Insurance, like national defense, is one of life's necessary evils. You need to balance your need for it with its cost. This chapter will attempt to show you what you need at a minimum. Your insurance agent will quote you costs. If he searches for the best prices and best policies for you (and he should), you will just have to accept them and buy them. Having an independent insurance agent who can deal with all insurance companies is your best way to get what you need in the way of insurance without getting more than you need.

INSURANCE TO PROTECT YOU

Life insurance. Sometimes this is described as insurance against the loss of a key employee by death. A key employee is one whose loss could be potentially fatal to the business. If two of you form a business, each one is probably a key employee. In order to determine "keyness" you have to fully understand the qualities that each brings to the business and understand how difficult it would be to replace those qualities with a replacement employee or partner in the event of loss. If you believe that replacement would be virtually impossible, then you must plan to use the insurance policy's death benefit for the purpose of liquidating the business. Liquidating means the paying off of liabilities, collection of all receivables, and the selling off of physical assets. This takes time and produces no income for the company.

That is why the insurance is needed. The surviving owner or heir still needs income during the liquidation.

If a key man dies and the company remains in business, the insurance death benefit helps cover costs while a replacement of the deceased person is sought. This process, also, obviously takes time and creates disruption. The death benefit paid by the insurer helps smooth the transition. Get key man life insurance and discuss with your insurance agent how to calculate how big a policy you will need.

The cost of life insurance premiums is dependent upon the age and health of the insured persons. This cost is part of your fixed overhead, as it does not change as business volume changes. **Term** life insurance rather than whole life insurance is the best approach for a business to insure its key people. It is the least expensive and the most flexible approach. **Whole life** policies gain in value as they age but a business wants all of its growth in working capital, not in life insurance.

Disability insurance. This should also be purchased for the key people because it provides them with income if they are prevented by accident or illness from working, regardless of whether the disability is job related. The business can then either eliminate or reduce the salary of the disabled person during the period of disability without the person suffering any financial loss. Get it.

Workmen's compensation insurance. This insurance protects the business from lawsuit by an employee injured on the job. (It also protects the employee, but more about that later). Comp is almost universally required by law, but even if it is not where you operate, get it. You must protect your employees from job related injury or illness. Comp premiums are based on payroll, the same as is social security. The bigger your payroll, the bigger your comp premium will be.

Insurers also rate businesses based on their safety records. They record each year how much premium for workmen's comp your company pays and compare it with the amount paid out in claims against your business for the same year. Insurers study this information in three year increments and then rate the businesses they insure on a basis of percentage. Each business starts out at a standard rating of 100% and thereafter is rated at a figure above or below that. If your average wage cost per hour is $20.00 and your standard rate is $10.00 premium for every $100.00 in wages, your weekly cost will work out like this.

Wages, 40 hours @ $20.00=$800.00

Comp premium @ $10%=$80.00

If you keep a safe working environment and your experience rating drops to 85%, then your premium for that employee's 40 hour week will drop to $68.00. So, you can see that employee safety, besides being morally right, also pays.

Casualty insurance. This is a grouping of insurance coverages which protects you from losses unrelated to your activities, such as theft, fire, flood, and wind damage. If you rent shop and office space, your landlord will normally insure the building, but not its contents. If its contents are your property, it would be wise to get some coverage. This type of coverage is fairly inexpensive.

INSURANCE THAT PROTECTS OTHERS FROM YOU

Workmen's compensation. This was described above as protecting your business from lawsuit by injured or sickened employees who could connect the injury or illness to the job. It also serves the purpose of providing medical costs and disability payments to the injured employees.

No matter how careful you may be in your efforts to keep your work environment safe, there will still be accidents and injuries. Sometimes these accidents will be caused wholly by the recklessness of employees, even perhaps in direct disobedience to your instructions. That, however, does not matter to workmen's comp. It is "no-fault" insurance. If the injury is lower back pain and the employee says he hurt himself lifting something on the job, then the insurer is required by law in most states to assume the injury to be job-related even though no proof is available.

Laws setting out requirements for workmen's compensation vary greatly from state to state. Some of them provide for very little disability income for employees prevented from working while recuperating. Find out for yourself what your state provides and then decide whether to do anything further to protect your employees.

Liability insurance. These policies protect others from damage you may do to their persons or property as a result of your business activities. More importantly, they also protect you from lawsuit by injured parties. Here is an example from my personal experience. Two of my painters were working on a new apartment building. Since the elevators were not yet in operation when we were painting it, we had to find our own way to raise our material to the various floors. What we chose to do was to hoist the five gallon pails of paint up the exterior of the building by rope and pulley hung from the balconies. Well, you guessed it. We dropped a full five gallon pail ten stories to the pavement below. Needless to say, it exploded. The mess extended over an amazingly large area.

There was no question about who was liable for the damage. We were. But our insurer paid all the costs of cleanup (less the deductible, of course). Get liability insurance.

Many of your customers (ALL of the sensible ones) will not hire you to do any jobs until you can show that you have workers' comp and liability insurance. This protects them from lawsuit brought by anyone injured financially or physically while on your customer's property. Most states place responsibility for public safety on the real estate owner (your customer). If a worker is injured or a passerby's car is hit by your paint overspray, the property owner is liable. That is why he insists that you protect him by way of insurance.

It is interesting to note that signs you put up saying "wet paint" are seen by the general public as a challenge. They believe that it is their civic duty to test the veracity of your signs. That means that you end up paying cleaning bills for their gloves, hats, and fur coats.

The message that you actually have insurance is called an insurance certificate. It is a form letter from your agent to your customer informing him of what coverage you have and promising to notify the customer immediately of any change in your insurance status. If you fail to pay the premium as agreed, your insurer will notify your customer and your customer, if he has half a brain, will cancel your job.

You can, of course, choose not to buy any insurance. If you do, here is what will become of you.

1. No commercial, institutional, or industrial customer will ever hire you.

2. No homeowner with any business sense will ever hire you.

3. No low income homeowner will ever hire you (or anybody else, for that matter, for lack of money to pay for the work).

4. That leaves for you a potential market of;

    a. Ignorant house owners who do not realize the risk they take when they hire you.

    b. Sleazy, semi-criminal types who deal in cash, keep no records, and expect the same from you. If you work for them, and wish to get paid, good luck!

If you take the uninsured approach to business, throw this book away now and get ready for a life of poverty in your golden years.

CHAPTER 11

OVERHEAD
....

You learned in earlier chapters that you need to know how much an hour's labor costs you. In this chapter I will explain how that is done and how you can update it each year. The whole purpose of course, is to price the work both to get the jobs and to make a profit on them. So, please refer to plate 9 (overhead spread sheet) .This is the most important of all my illustrations. *Please note: this illustration was designed when the dollar was stronger than it is now and therefore wage levels were lower than they are now. Ignore that. It does not affect the validity of this system.*

Notice that the year columns to the right, starting with column D, hold the information you entered from your P&L statement each year plus the calculations made by the computer so that you can make use of the information you entered from your books. (I showed you the format of a P&L statement in chapter 4). My personal preference is to place the most recent year in the leftmost column but that is not terribly important. You can place it wherever you wish.

The leftmost year column on the page is entered from your P&L statement once each year at the end of your fiscal year. Your bookkeeping should be set up by an accountant, It should comprise a payroll journal, a general journal, and a ledger. This is standard procedure and easily understood once it is properly set up. So, let us assume that your books are in order and you have completed your third year in business in 1993. When your

PLATE 9

A B	C	D	E	F
1 INFORMATION FOR FUN & PROFIT	DESCRIPTION	3dYEAR	2dYEAR	1st YEAR
2 YOU FILL IN THE FIGURES		1993	1992	1991
3 GROSS INCOME	TOTAL SALES	510345	465321	401291
4 SALARIES	FIXED OVERHEAD	42000	42000	42000
5 INTEREST LONG TERM	FIXED OVERHEAD	1000	1200	1500
6 FICA EXECUTIVES	FIXED OVERHEAD	3213	3213	3213
7 ALL INSURANCE COSTS, EXECUTIVES	FIXED OVERHEAD	2389	2341	2310
8 TELEPHONE AND ADVERTISING	FIXED OVERHEAD	4131	3810	4501
9 CHARITABLE DONATIONS	FIXED OVERHEAD	250	300	225
10 ENTERTAINMENT	FIXED OVERHEAD	100		
11 VEHICLE MAINTENANCE	FIXED OVERHEAD	2748	1745	1528
12 VEHICLE LICENSE AND INSURANCE	FIXED OVERHEAD	2800	2900	3210
13 VEHICLE DEPRECIATION	FIXED OVERHEAD	2200	2900	3400
14 EAQUIPMENT DEPRECIATION	FIXED OVERHEAD	3900	4200	4500
15 EQUIPMENT INSURANCE	FIXED OVERHEAD	650	650	650
16 SHOP RENT, UTILITIES, AND TAXES	FIXED OVERHEAD	7000	6950	5950
17 DEPREC., LEASEHOLD IMPROVEMENTS	FIXED OVERHEAD		500	500
18 OFFICE EXPENSE	FIXED OVERHEAD	2243	1937	1866
19 LEGAL AND AUDIT EXPENSE	FIXED OVERHEAD	310	310	659
20 DUES AND SUBSCRIPTIONS	FIXED OVERHEAD	150	150	150
21 MISCELLANEOUS EXPENSE	FIXED OVERHEAD	1322	1111	997
22 TOTAL GENERAL OVERHEAD	all above fixed overhead	76404	76217	78249
23 TOTAL HOURS ESTIMATING	self explanatory	1580	1784	1649
24 WAGE COST FOR ESTIMATING	FIXED OVERHEAD	18100	21408	20365
25 WORKERS' COMP., ESTIMATING	FIXED OVERHEAD	1810	2141	2037
26 LIABILITY INSURANCE, ESTIMATING	FIXED OVERHEAD	805	1019	999
27 FICA, ESTIMATING	FIXED OVERHEAD	1424	1638	1558
28 UNEMPLOYMENT INS., ESTIMATING	FIXED OVERHEAD	905	1019	999
29 HEALTH INSURANCE, ESTIMATING	FIXED OVERHEAD	1230	1123	1067
30 TOTAL COST, ESTIMATING	total above 6 lines	24274	28348	27025
31 COST PER HOUR, ESTIMATING	mean	15.36	15.89	16.39
32 TOTAL FIXED OVERHEAD FOR YEAR	grand total fixed o/h	100678	104385	105274
33 OTHER NONPRODUCTIVE HOURS (ONPH)	down time hours	798	508	591
34 WAGE COST ONPH	VARIABLE OVERHEAD	9100	5080	5781
35 WORKERS' COMP., ONPH	VARIABLE OVERHEAD	910	506	578
36 LIABILITY INSURANCE, ONPH	VARIABLE OVERHEAD	455	254	289
37 FICA ONPH	VARIABLE OVERHEAD	896	389	442
38 UNEMPLOYMENT INS., ONPH	VARIABLE OVERHEAD	455	508	578
39 HEALTH INSURANCE, ONPH	VARIABLE OVERHEAD	810	736	821
40 TOTAL COST, ONPH	total above 6 lines	12228	7475	8489
41 COST/HOUR, ONPH	mean	15.32	14.71	14.36
42 TOTAL PRODUCTIVE HOURS FOR YEAR	direct hours on jobs	13121	11377	10002
43 WAGE COST, PRODUCTIVE HOURS	DIRECT COST	162589	135273	114023
44 WORKERS' COMP., PRODUCTIVE HOURS	VARIABLE OVERHEAD	16259	13527	11402
45 LIABILITY INS., PRODUCTIVE HOURS	VARIABLE OVERHEAD	8130	8764	5701
46 FICA, PRODUCTIVE HOURS	VARIABLE OVERHEAD	12438	10348	8123
47 UNEMPLOYMENT INS., PROD. HOURS	VARIABLE OVERHEAD	8130	8764	5701
48 HEALTH INS., PRODUCTIVE HOURS	VARIABLE OVERHEAD	13705	11002	9399
49 INTEREST SHORT TERM	VARIABLE OVERHEAD	3122	2000	1348
50 HAZARDOUS WASTE	VARIABLE OVERHEAD	2911	2142	1311
51 EQUIPMENT MAINTENANCE	VARIABLE OVERHEAD	997	137	429
52 SMALL TOOL EXPENSE	VARIABLE OVERHEAD	18756	14333	10492
53 SUM OF TWO PRIOR LINES	often useful subtotal	17753	14470	10921
54 PRIOR LINE COST/PRODUCTIVE HOUR	often useful ratio	1.35	1.27	1.09
55 TOTAL VARIABLE OVERHEAD, YEAR	VARIABLE OVERHEAD	94674	74493	63495
56 VARIABLE O/H PER PRODUCTIVE HOUR	at mean hourly wage	7.22	6.55	6.35
57 FIXED O/H PER PRODUCTIVE HOUR	at any wage level	7.67	9.17	10.53
58 WAGES PER PRODUCTIVE HOUR	at mean hourly wage	12.39	11.89	11.40
69 TOTAL COST PER PRODUCTIVE HOUR	at mean hourly wage	27.28	27.61	28.27
60 DOLLAR SALES PER PRODUCTIVE HOUR	interesting but useless	38.9	40.9	40.12
61 VARIABLE O/H AS % OF WAGES	vital information	58.20%	55.10%	55.70%
62 LINE 61 LESS LINE 53	useful in pricing overtime	47.30%	44.40%	46.10%

books are balanced for the year you can then analyze your overhead using this spread sheet. Follow down the 1993 column with me. The gross sales figure is the year's income. It is the first figure on your annual statement of profit and loss. Just enter it in the 1993 column. (I have done all the entries for you in this example). The second line, officers salaries, comes from your P&L statement also, and so does long term interest.

FICA for executives is calculated by the computer as 7.65% of the $42,000 you paid out in salaries. The amount is entered automatically because you previously told the computer (when you set up this spreadsheet) to do so. What you told it to do was to multiply any figure you entered in the officers' salaries line by .0765 and enter the product in that space, rounded off to the nearest dollar. All of the items of FIXED OVERHEAD involving insurance costs may show up on the P&L in a combined manner. If they do, you will have to study the policies to figure out how much money to allocate to each insurance line on this spread sheet. If you do, the easiest approach is to invite your insurance agent to help you. For him it is easy. For you it is difficult.

The entries from telephone through equipment depreciation are all copied directly from figures on your P&L statement.

Equipment insurance is one of those figures you get from your ever helpful insurance agent.

Shop rent and utilities are direct entries from the P&L.

Leasehold improvements are defined as improvements you make to the property which you rent. These improvements are money spent to make long term investment in your rented facilities (with the landlord's approval, of course). The purpose of improvements to the property of others is to enhance the profitability of your business, naturally. You would not do it without a lease long enough for you to regain the money through depreciating the cost on your income tax. The length of term of depreciation is for you and your accountant to decide. That decision needs to be an amalgam of wise business decisions as well as tax law decisions. The IRS will let you depreciate for tax purposes faster than the real depreciation but it will not let you get away with murder and take all the depreciation in one year for something which will be of value to you for six years.

The next four items, office through miscellaneous, are direct entries from the P&L.

Total general overhead (line 22) is calculated automatically by the computer by adding up the fixed overhead items previously entered.

Now we enter the second phase of fixed overhead which I lump together as estimating cost. You could consider estimating as a variable overhead if you choose to. I do not so choose because you must keep on estimating all year long, regardless of whether you land any jobs. Also, estimating costs do not vary with volume of business as directly as do other costs. The first line, total hours estimating, is derived from your 52 weekly payroll recap sheets (plate 16). Each week's recap of labor shows how many hours were spent on estimates that week. Adding them up will give you the figure to enter in the "total hours estimating" line.

Wage cost for estimating comes from the same 52 forms. Just add them up and enter the sum on that line.

All the insurance items in the estimating phase must be figured out from insurance premiums as you did earlier for officers' insurance costs. Here is where you again consult with your insurance agent.

FICA for estimating labor is again entered by the computer itself because it was programmed in advance to do the mathematics. It also automatically enters the total cost for estimates.

The next line, cost per hour estimating, is not really necessary but it is fun to look at from year to year. It requires no effort because the computer does the work, so you might as well have it in there. It is calculated by dividing the total dollar cost for estimating by the total hours involved.

When creating your own spreadsheet, you could very well leave out this line.

Total fixed overhead for the year is calculated by the computer simply by adding together the total general overhead and the total estimating overhead. This is a dollar figure and in the example I have created for year 1993, it is $100,678, (the sum of $76,404 and $24,274).

The next nine lines deal with VARIABLE OVERHEAD caused by down time. Down time can be defined as labor cost spent on non-productive work. It is work that cannot be billed to a customer. Tidying the shop, fixing a flat tire, replacing the packings in a pump, mollifying a disgruntled customer, looking for lost ladders. All these actions and millions more, if done by hourly employees would be classified as down time. Down time is inevitable. You will have some every year in which you are in business. The trick is to keep the amount of it under reasonable control. The best way to do that is to know how much down time you have each year and compare it with your experience of previous years. These nine lines give you the power to do just that. Follow along.

The line "other non-productive hours" is derived by adding the totals of the 52 weeks' worth of ONPH hours from the

WEEKLY PAYROLL RECAPITULATION sheet (plate 18). Enter it in this space.

"Wage cost ONPH" means the total number of dollars you spent during the year for down time wages. ONPH stands for other non productive hours (other than estimating hours). This is arrived at by adding 52 weeks' worth of "no job" wages from the 52 WEEKLY PAYROLL RECAPITULATION sheets.

Four of the next five lines will be entered by you with the help of your ever present and ever helpful insurance agent. They are all insurance items. The fifth, FICA ONPH is automatically entered by the computer.

Total cost ONPH is calculated by the computer by adding the six lines above.

"Cost per hour ONPH" is automatically entered and is not a necessary bit of information but it is definitely interesting. In this sample the down time cost per hour is $15.32.

You have now recorded all your overhead for the year. Now, for that to mean anything, you have to compare it with your actual productive hours of labor. All of the next information you enter will be actual billable (productive) labor. You also have to compare it with your experience in previous years. That is why every fiscal year is shown on the same spread sheet.

The next entry is "total productive hours". These are the hours in which your employees actually worked on your jobs. You gather this information from the 52 WEEKLY PAYROLL RECAPITULATION sheets.

In my example I show 13,121 hours of direct job labor and in the next line I show a direct dollar cost of $162,589 for these hours (also taken from the RECAPITULATION).

The next five items are four insurance costs and FICA. Again FICA is automatically calculated and the other four items are a portion of your total insurance cost and you need your agent to help you enter the correct amounts.

"Interest, short term" is a figure you take directly from your P&L. It is the cost of money you borrow to run your jobs. This is variable overhead because if you have no jobs you have no need to borrow working capital.

Hazardous waste disposal could be a direct job expense if you can tie it to a specific job in a specific amount, but that is difficult to do in this business. Most painting contractors end up with leftover materials which are hazardous but they do not know which jobs they came from. Therefore I suggest you call it an item of variable overhead. It seems to me that it costs roughly the same per man-hour of productive labor, regardless of the number of man-hours actually worked. If you find that it varies per hour depending on what kind of work you do, you can easily call it a direct job cost under the account, "subcontract". If you choose to do that, it will not show up in your overhead. If, for example, you specialize in removal of lead paint, then hazardous waste removal will be an unusually large feature of your bookkeeping and should be handled whichever way works best for you as long as you do it consistently one way or the other (as overhead or as direct job cost under "subcontracting").

"Equipment maintenance", if done by an outside vendor, is obviously an item of variable overhead. If you do it with your own employees it will show up as down time labor. In either case it will be accurately entered on this spread sheet as variable overhead. This figure comes directly from your P&L.

"Small tool expense" also comes directly from the P&L. This is the money you spent during the year on tools that rapidly wear out. This is a larger figure for painters than it is for most other trades because the tools are expensive and they wear out very quickly. Carpenters and masons, for example, provide their own hand tools at no cost to the employer. The contractor employing these two trades only supplies power tools and other equipment as part of his overhead.

The "sum of two previous lines" is added automatically by the computer. I only put it in to help you calculate this dual expense separately from other variable expenses because sometimes you will need to calculate an hourly rate to charge a customer for work done at night or on weekends. Obviously, even if you pay your painters premium wages for working off of normal hours, the cost per hour for these two items will still remain the same. See the example later in this chapter.

That cost per hour of productive labor for tools and equipment maintenance is automatically calculated by the computer in the next line called "prior line cost/productive hr".

The next four lines are all automatic calculations and they are the answers you need for pricing your work. They are the whole purpose in doing this overhead spreadsheet. The "total variable overhead for year" is the sum of all the variable overhead items you entered above.

The "variable overhead per productive hour" is the variable overhead cost for one hour's labor at the mean wage scale you paid during the year. In this sample year, the mean wage was $12.39 per hour. This shows up two lines hence.

The "fixed overhead per productive hour" is the fixed overhead cost per hour for any productive hour worked by any employee at any rate of pay. This is important for you to understand. A person getting $20.00 per hour costs you no more in fixed overhead than does a person getting the minimum wage. For this reason, highly skilled and highly paid individuals are a better buy than low skill-low wage employees.

The "total cost per productive hour" is the total cost per hour for the employee getting the mean wage in this particular year, namely $12.39 per hour. You will see that the $12.39 person costs a total of $27.28 per hour in this sample.

The final line shows you how much sales you generated per hour worked on your jobs. This can be useful in comparing one year's production against another's. It is simply the total sales divided by the total number of productive hours. The computer does the work. All you do is reap the benefits.

> You will use this spread sheet to answer any pricing question you may have. For example; 1. For what rate should I sell the services of my highest paid painter to a customer who wants him on an hourly basis ? Here is how you do it. Assume his pay is $17.50. You all ready know that his fixed overhead cost is $7.67 because every employee's fixed cost is $7.67. From line 62 you see that variable overhead is 58% of wages and that comes to $10.15 (17.50x.58). Now find the sum of wages, fixed overhead, and variable overhead for this particular employee and you have the total cost per hour. You will find that it comes to $35.32 . If you and your customer agree on cost plus 10% as the selling price, add $3.53 and sell the guy for $38.85 per hour.

If your lowest paid employee is an unskilled laborer at $5.00 per hour, his selling price at cost plus 10% would be

$5.00 wage

7.67 fixed o/h

2.90 var. o/h

15.57 total cost

.56 profit

$20.03 selling price per hour

2. If you need to know how much to carry per hour in your estimate of the cost of a contract price job you are pricing, then you will use the figure from line 60 ($27.28). It is the cost for your average painter. When you are finished totaling the estimated cost for the entire job, including labor, material, subcontracts, equipment rental and anything else which may be pertinent to this job, then add a profit.

3. How do I calculate the cost per hour for work done at premium pay? This is slightly more complicated than the above stuff but well worth doing. Assume your average painter's wages for this example.

$12.39 straight time wage from line 59

6.20 premium pay at time and one half   subtotal 18.59 total direct hourly wage (average)

7.67 fixed overhead

8.74 variable overhead from line 62(not line 61)

1.35 from line 53

$36.35 total cost per hour

This gives you the most accurate estimate of hourly cost that you can reasonably expect. You will probably find over the years that it is far more accurate than anything you ever had before. I certainly hope so, after all this work.

Please notice the interesting fact that, even though the wages on overtime are multiplied by 1.5, the total cost increases by a factor of only 1.33. This is because fixed over-head and tools and equipment use do not change, regard-less of wage rates.

If you wish to see the formulas I installed in the compu-ter's spread sheet program for this study, see plate 12 in the illustrations.

PLATE 12

INFORMATION FOR FUN AND PROFIT	DESCRIPTION	FORMULAS USED
GROSS INCOME	TOTAL SALES	
EXECUTIVE SALARIES	fixed overhead	
INTEREST LONG TERM	fixed overhead	
FICA, EXECUTIVES	fixed overhead	=D4*.0675
EXECS	fixed overhead	
ADVERTISING	fixed overhead	
CHARITY DONATIONS	fixed overhead	
ENTERTAINMENT	fixed overhead	
VEHICLE MAINTENANCE	fixed overhead	
VEHICLE LICENSE, INSURANCE	fixed overhead	
VEHICLE DEPRECIATION	fixed overhead	
DEPRECIATION	fixed overhead	
EQUIPMENT INSURANCE	fixed overhead	
SHOP RENT, UTILITIES, TAXES	fixed overhead	
DEPRECIATION OF LEASEHOLD IMPROVEMENTS	fixed overhead	
OFFICE EXPENSES	fixed overhead	
LEGAL AND AUDIT EXPENSE	fixed overhead	
DUES AND SUBSCRIPTIONS	fixed overhead	
MISCELLANEOUS EXPENSE	fixed overhead	
TOTAL GENERAL OVERHEAD		=SUM(D4:D21)

ESTIMATING		
WAGES, ESTIMATING	fixed overhead	
ESTIMATING	fixed overhead	
ESTIMATING	fixed overhead	
FICA ESTIMATING	fixed overhead	=D24*.0675
UNEMPLOYMENT INS. ESTIMATING	fixed overhead	
HEALTH INS. ESTIMATING	fixed overhead	
TOTAL COST ESTIMATING	fixed overhead	=SUM(D24:D29)
COST/HOUR ESTIMATING		=D30/D23
TOTAL FIXED OVERHEAD FOR THE YEAR		=SUM(D22+D30)
OTHER NON-PRODUCTIVE HOURS (ONPH)	down time hours	
WAGES, ONPH	variable overhead	
WORKERS COMP ONPH	variable overhead	
LIABILITY INS. ONPH	variable overhead	
FICA ONPH	variable overhead	=D34*.0765
ONPH	variable overhead	
HEALTH INS. ONPH	variable overhead	
TOTAL COST ONPH	variable overhead	=SUM(D34:D39)
COST PER HOUR ONPH		=D40/D33
TOTAL PRODUCTIVE HOURS FOR THE YEAR	direct job labor	
WAGES, PRODUCTIVE HOURS	direct cost	
WORKERS COMP, PRODUCTIVE HOURS	variable overhead	
LIABILITY INS., PRODUCTIVE HOURS	variable overhead	
FICA, PRODUCTIVE HOURS	variable overhead	=D43*.0765
UNEMPLOYMENT INS. PRODUCTIVE HOURS	variable overhead	
HEALTH INS. PRODUCTIVE HOURS	variable overhead	
INTEREST, SHORT TERM	variable overhead	
HAZARDOUS WASTE	variable overhead	
EQUIPMENT MAINTENANCE	variable overhead	
SMALL TOOL EXPENSE	variable overhead	

SUM OF TWO PRIOR LINES	useful subtotal	
TOOLS & EQUIP. MAINT. PER PRODUCTIVE HOUR	useful ratio	=D53/D42
TOTAL VARIABLE OVERHEAD FOR THE YEAR	variable overhead	=D40+SUM(D44:D52)
VARIABLE OVERHEAD PER PRODUCTIVE HOUR	at average wage	=D55/D42
FIXED OVERHEAD PER PRODUCTIVE HOUR	fixed overhead	=D32/D42
WAGES PER PRODUCTIVE HOUR	average wage	=D43/D42
TOTAL COST PER PRODUCTIVE HOUR	at average wage	=SUM(D56:D58)
DOLLAR SALES PER PRODUCTIVE HOUR	interesting ratio	=D3/D42
VARIABLE OVERHEAD AS A PERCENT OF WAGES	vital information	=D55/D43
LINE 61 LESS LINE 53	useful for pricing overtime work	=(D55-D53)/D43

Now imagine that you have a fussy customer with deep pockets who wants to hire you on a basis of cost plus 10%. He might balk at your quoted hourly rate because he does not understand how you arrived at it. If this happens, cheerfully show him your overhead printout. It is a great selling tool and will convince him that you really know what you are doing and that your quoted rate really does pay you a profit of ten percent and no more. If he is really sharp, he may say to you, "why should I pay you for the estimating portion of fixed overhead when this job I offer you is cost plus and therefore costs you nothing for estimating ?"

You will then have two response choices. They are, "Take it or leave it." or "OK, you're right. I'll reduce the price."

Whatever way you use this overhead spread sheet, you will probably find it to be your most valuable business document. *Do not fail to enter it each year.*

You are now able to figure out the value of your WORK IN PROCESS which I promised to explain way back in chapter four. You may recall that it shows up on your BALANCE SHEET (plate 21) as a current asset. To calculate the value of work in process you first establish what date applies to your balance sheet and use that date as the value date for WIP. Then you use the format on the job cost recapitulation form (plate 14), even though the job is not yet complete. You can add up the cost of a job at any time during its process and you can do it any number of times. Just don't bother using the space labeled "profit" until the final time you recap the job (when it is all finished and all costs have been entered into your bookkeeping).

Now get this and get it right. Work in process is the value of work not yet billed to your customers. If you have billed it, your books will show the value of completed work as an asset under accounts receivable and you must not also show the same work as another asset.

Sometimes you will have occasion to bill out a job in monthly requisitions for payment. If you are in the middle of a job of that sort when the date arrives to do a profit and loss statement, and you forget to bill the customer that month, then the cost of the work done that month and that month only will be entered on your balance sheet as work in process.

If you are doing a lot of small jobs on a cost plus basis in any given month, the work in process figure is likely to be fairly high because you must wait for all material invoices to come in before recapping the jobs and sending bills. It is embarrassing to bill out a cost plus job more than once because an invoice arrived after you billed it the first time. It makes you look less than perfect. I did that once and my face was very red.

Now that you have read column C from top to bottom and learned everything you wish to know about your over-head in 1993, let me direct your attention horizontally so that you can compare each line's information in 1993 with the two previous years. If your volume of business is growing, as shown in this sample, each line's entry should also grow, in general. This is not a hard and fast rule though. Look at line 13. You are losing less value in vehicles in 1993 than in '92 and '91 but that only means that your trucks are wearing out. Now look at line 17. It shows that you had no leasehold depreciation in 1993, even though you did the two previous years. That's probably a good thing because presumably your leasehold improvements are still in place and working for you, even if they are all paid for and all depreciated.

Line 33 is important to look at each year. If your total down time hours remain roughly the same each year in relation to your total of productive hours, you need not be alarmed. But if you see a spurt upward one year, it is a warning that your administration is getting sloppy and you must seek to regain control of your jobs and your shop.

Line 54 is also an indicator of how good your control is. In this example, 1993 and 1992 are very close together and may indicate nothing more than inflation from one year to the next. But 1991's expense was quite a bit lower. This could be a danger signal, so investigate. Why was there such a difference ? Look up to lines 51 and 52 and you will find the answer in line 51. Your maintenance cost is spiking upward in '93, a possible indication that some of your equipment is aging to the point where it should be replaced. As line 14 (equipment depreciation) diminishes, line 52 (equipment maintenance) increases. That makes sense does it not?

Line 57 in this sample spreadsheet shows you that fixed overhead per productive hour is on a three year decline. Since this hypothetical business began in 1991 with little business and improved its business volume each year, this is the result you should expect. A peek at line 42 tells you the story. Do not expect your fixed overhead per productive hour to continue on a downward trend forever, however. When you hit your optimum volume of business, it should then settle down and remain fairly stable from year to year.

You now have the power to control the destiny of your business. All you need now is the will.

CHAPTER 12

YOUR COMPUTER
....

To start up your business you need a modest size computer capable of handling software to operate data base (such
as the unit cost records), word processing (letters etc.), and
spread sheet for analysis work (such as your annual overhead
study and your estimating recap sheets). In the future you
may also wish to computerize bookkeeping also.

Computers are inexpensive enough now so that with a
modest outlay you can have everything you will need for
years. I recommend that you get a desk model because a
monitor large enough to display a large spreadsheet is very
handy. Every computer built nowadays has plenty of memory for what you will need. You should also have a printer
and scanner. Nowadays you can buy a combination fax,
printer, scanner, and copier in one machine for surprisingly
little money.

For software I recommend a multi-purpose program that
will incorporate spread sheet, data base, and word processing all in one program. There are many excellent ones on
the market now and they keep improving all the time. All
the illustrations in this book are done on Microsoft Word
or Microsoft Excel for text and spread sheet and Microsoft
Works for data base (unit cost records). not because they
are best but simply because they are nearly universally

recognized. If you decide to keep books on computer, add an accounting program which can do job cost recording as well as payroll, journals, and ledgers. It must also do statements of profit and loss, trial balance, and net worth statements. In other words, go whole hog. It does not cost very much.

CHAPTER 13

THE BREAK EVEN POINT
···

Warning! Before reading this chapter, steel yourself to read it, enjoy it if possible, learn something maybe, BUT do not do anything with the insight you have gained from it. Any use of the break even point must be deferred until you have many years in business and have had time to get everything under perfect control. Then, if you have dutifully kept up your overhead records for every year in business using the format in illustration plate 9, then and only then should you think about using the break even point as a business strategy. All right, are you sufficiently warned? If so, read on and I will tell you what it is and how it can be used. Please refer now to plate 9, overhead spread sheet.

Line 32 shows you in dollars, how much your fixed overhead costs you each year. In the case of this example, the most recent year's fixed overhead was $100,678 and the fixed overhead varied only slightly from year to year for the three years it was recorded.

Now direct your attention to line 42 which shows how many productive or billable hours your employees worked in the same three years. You can see that, while fixed overhead remained fairly stable, productive hours kept rising over the three year period. That's good. It must follow that the fixed overhead cost per hour must be shrinking. To find out

exactly how much, see line 57. The year 1993 was this contractor's third year in business. He can guess at what volume
of business he will do in 1994 but his only source of knowledge upon which to base that guess is this spread sheet. If
it contained ten years' worth of records instead of three, his
guesswork would be much more accurate. Remember, I told
you in an earlier chapter that if you fly by the seat of your
pants you will crash.

Anyway, let us say that he predicts 14,000 productive
hours for 1994 and that his fixed overhead will increase to
$108,000. Then he looks at line 58 (you do it, too) and sees
that his employees' average direct wage rate per productive hour is on a steady rise, so he decides to predict that
his rate of pay will average $12.80 per hour in 1994. So he
divides $108,000 (estimated annual cost of fixed overhead)
by his estimate of 14,000 productive hours and gets $7.71
as his estimated fixed overhead cost per hour. He also estimates that the variable overhead, which is tied to wages, will
remain at 58% (see line 62). That all adds up to a total cost
per hour of

Wages	$12.80
fixed o/h	7.71
Variable o/h	7.42 (58% of $12.80)
Total cost/ hr.	$27.93

Now the scene shifts to 1994 and ten months into the
fiscal year. Our contractor notices that after ten months his
volume is greater than expected and he reaches 14,000 productive hours two months before the year ends. THAT POINT
AT WHICH HE REACHES 14,000 IS THE BREAK EVEN POINT.
Theoretically, he cannot lose money for the year. All his jobs

were calculated at an hourly cost of $27.93 and they all took exactly the amount of hours he estimated they would (He apparently has celestial connections).

This means that the 14,000 productive hours, for which he got paid $7.71 each for fixed overhead have returned him $108,000. Presto, he discovers that his fixed overhead for the year is all ready paid for and there are two months to go. Theoretically, he could close the business down for two months and still break even. In fact he has three choices. They are;

1. close down for two months

2. continue working and making an extra $7.71 per hour in profit

3. bid on a two month job at a cost per hour $7.71 less than usual in order to underbid the competition and keep working

Option #1 is crazy. We will discuss it no further. Option #2 is nearly always the only sensible thing to do. Option #3, though, is fascinating.

Let's try this scenario. Our contractor is requested to bid on a six week job for which he has enough manpower. He has very little other work for the last two months. The competition for this plum of a job is very strong. He could bid the job at a total cost per hour of $20.22 ($12.80 wages and $7.42 variable overhead) because his fixed overhead for the year has all ready been earned. That would obviously give him a tremendous competitive advantage. That, my dear reader, is the lure of Break Even Point.

I strongly recommend that you wait until you have been in business successfully for at least ten years before you try such an approach. You need the accumulated data from your overhead spread sheet for at least that long. Also, it is risky. You could compound the problem of a bad mistake in estimating by underpricing the work , too. A more conservative approach to being as competitive as possible is to keep your volume growing steadily year by year while keeping a close watch on your fixed overhead, thereby reducing your fixed overhead cost per productive hour year by year. That way you will always be competitive but never in danger of business failure caused by the most common mistake of all. That mistake is not knowing your costs. Remember the formula. Fly X (seat + pants)=crash.

CHAPTER 14

DISASTER AVOIDANCE
·······································

The disaster I refer to is the financial disaster caused by one or more jobs losing tons of money all in one fiscal year. EVERY business created by humans will sooner or later suffer from a financial disaster. Chrysler Corporation's disaster was so great that it took the financial backing of the United States of America to save it. Realistically, you, the new painting contractor cannot expect such help, so prepare to weather disasters, contain them, and be vigilant to avoid them.

Disasters can be caused by mistakes you make, bad luck, and fraud. Mistakes you make can be avoided by religiously following the advice so generously marbled throughout the other chapters of this book. Bad luck cannot be controlled but you can be protected against most of it through your various kinds of insurance. Fraud is something you need to be conscious of all your business life. In general, you can avoid the sleazebags by doing business only with people of proven integrity, but, now and then a deadbeat will appear and surprise you by depriving you of money you earned.

Spotting deadbeats and avoiding being entrapped by them is one activity that makes business a real pleasure. Likewise, failure to avoid them brings great misery. Losing money because of your own mistakes is bad enough, but to lose it through a deadbeat's fraud is often unbearable. If you let it happen often enough, it can turn you into a bitter curmudgeon.

A deadbeat is a person who borrows or buys from you with no intention of repayment or, at least, no intention of timely or full payment. For that reason, he needs to fool you into thinking that he can be trusted. Here are some tried and true symptoms of the disease and some antidotes you can use.

Symptom. He produces an elaborate business "front" which is designed to make you think he has a successful, going concern with which you should be glad to do business. He is the founder of the business, dresses like a trial lawyer, drives a flashy, expensive car, has a fancy office with a pulchritudinous receptionist, and is under thirty. The only two things on his desktop are his feet.

Antidote. Check his credit and his references. Talk to his customers and vendors. Most likely, he is trying to fool you.

Symptom. He drops names of successful, powerful people and implies that he has close relationships with them. His office will probably have an "ego wall" covered with pictures of himself shaking hands with politicians.

Antidote. Question him closely about those relationships. If he takes offense, you then know he is a fraud. An honest person will not take offense.

Symptom. He talks of large debts owed to him by rich and well known people (soon to be collected in full, of course) or of court decisions in his favor (also soon to be collected, of course). His implication is that the money to pay you is a sure thing.

Antidote. Your inference should be that if he does not pay, he will blame someone else for failing to pay him, thus relieving him of responsibility to pay you. Get the money secured in advance or don't work for him.

Symptom. He hurries you into doing a job for him because "time is of the essence" before you have a chance to check his credit. His motive is to trap you into investing your assets in his favor before you learn that payment will at best be very slow, so that you will "send good money chasing bad" just to protect your investment. He will provide references while at the same time pressing you to start the work while you check his references later. The references will be dead, moved with no forwarding address, without listed telephone, or maybe even all of the above. He hopes you will be working on his job for a while before you catch on.

Antidote. Check first. If you failed to do that and started his job, as soon as you think you are being tricked, stop working and confront him. The last thing he wants is an unfinished job. If you finish the work you have no power over him.

Symptom. He flatters you profusely with "all the good things he has heard about you", and how he is honored to be able to do business with you etc. etc. He oozes self -confidence, treats you as a confidante on your first acquaintance, and offers you a drink of top shelf liquor from a hidden cabinet in his private office.

Antidote. Run like hell.

Symptom. He talks you into doing a small job. You take a chance and do the job and he pays surprisingly promptly. He implies but is careful not to say, that he always pays like that.

Antidote. Check his references before you do the next job.

Now, all of the examples above describe people for whom you might perform a service and not get paid, but you can also get hurt financially by fraudulent vendors. If you hire a subcontractor to do a job for you, do not pay any money in advance. If you place an order for material, do not pay any money in advance. The only exception to this rule which can prudently be made is for an extraordinary job requiring a large deposit of cash for the vendor to buy special and expensive material. If such a deposit is required, be sure you can trust your vendor and get verification that the money was used for its intended purpose. (A simple way to accomplish this goal is to write your check to both the vendor and his manufacturer). Then the only risk left is that the manufacturer of the special material might go bankrupt after accepting your vendor's order and your cash.

Well, you have to take some risk !

Is there ever, you might ask, any justification for working for a known deadbeat ? My answer to that is NO. However, you might wish to consider if there is justification for working for a customer who is financially shaky but honest. That question can be answered with some arithmetic.

First, refer again to plate 9, the overhead spread sheet. This is still a hypothetical painting contractor's three year record of overhead costs.

Using the column for the most recent year, you find on line 57 that the fixed overhead per productive hour was $7.67. Line 59 shows you that the total cost per productive hour was $27.28. If you decide not to work for the deadbeat or the shaky honest guy and you have no other work, then theoretically you are losing $7.67 for every hour of work you decide to forego. If you do the work and do not get paid, you lose $27.28 per hour plus 100% of the cost of materials. Which amount is better to lose; $27.28 or $7.67 ? The answer is obvious but consideration is still due because you might be able to arrange with your customer to secure your contract amount somehow before starting the job. There are many ways this can be done and your banker is probably the person whose brain to pick if the customer agrees to do it. If the customer balks, then just forego the job. $27.28 lost is worse than $7.67 lost.

If you take the job offered you by the shaky honest guy, calculate the risk and add something to the price. For example, if you are certain of getting paid but expect payment to take nine months, add to your price the cost of interest on the money owed. If you are only semi-certain of getting paid, figure the odds, and add to your price a bonus for the risk. This sort of risk juggling is not a science. It is an art. Be an artist if you wish, but be very careful.

Disasters can be delivered to you by your well heeled and reputable customer also. One of the worst in my experience was caused by the customer of our customer. Our customer was a general contractor who had been hired by a college to remodel one of its buildings. The contract for painting was extremely elaborate with multiple colors and kinds of paint. Some of the paints were multi-colored products which had to be sprayed, adjacent to trim work which had to be brushed. The general contractor had to do very complex structural and mechanical work before getting to the finishes, and the timing of the job was unrealistically tight. The college, personified by its director of physical plant, promised to cooperate to the fullest in order to achieve its scheduling goal. He did not do so, and the general contractor could not force him to do so. Needless to say, the job was a madhouse on which every subcontractor lost money and the general contractor lost really big money. The college got its job done well and on time but only at the expense of all the building trades businesses that worked there.

That director of physical plant of that college has developed such a reputation in the building trades that, rumor has it, every bid he gets now has a 20% additional factor added in to cover the cost of his unreasonable demands and lack of cooperation with his contractors. That may be good news now but it will never make up for the disasters he caused.

We could have avoided that disaster but we did not. We could have walked away and not bid the job. If we had, we would have abjured a possible net profit of $1,000. But did we? No, we took a chance on a long shot at a tight profit margin and instead took a loss of $11,000. We wanted the job because it was challenging and prestigious, so we ignored the warning signs and went ahead with it anyway. You can do the same if you wish, but I do not recommend it.

CHAPTER 15

HOW TO CALCULATE THE VALUE

OF WORK IN PROCESS

At the end of each month or quarter you will need to know whether or not you are making profit. The balance sheet prepared by your accountant from your books will give you an accurate picture except for one missing ingredient. That ingredient is the value of the work you have under way for which you have incurred expenses and for which you have not yet billed a customer. Because of this very common situation, your books show expenses not balanced by income, thus making your business look financially weaker than it really is.

The solution is simple. Give your accountant an estimate of the value of the work in process and he will incorporate it into the balance sheet as shown on plate 21. The estimate is quick and easy to do using the job cost records. Refer to plates 14 and 17. Plate 17 is the standard job cost record which you enter each week. Plate 14 is printed on the back side of each job cost record form and is normally only used once, at the end of the job.

Let's assume first that the job you have not yet billed for the period in question is a new one and has therefore not been partially billed before. In that case, simply transfer the information from the cost record (plate 17) to the job cost recap form (plate 14) and do the necessary multiplying so as to get a total cost. Do not proceed beyond the line called "total cost". That figure is the value of the work in process on that job.

Now let's assume that you are part way through a big job for which you have all ready sent bills for partial payment (called "requisition" on the cost sheet). The procedure is the same as above with one small added step. Once you arrive at the total cost of the job to date, simply subtract from that the amount you have previously billed (requisitioned). Those earlier bills have all ready been entered into your books as accounts receivable and income, so you cannot use that money again as work in process without artificially inflating your net worth.

Once you have found the value of work in process for each job that has some, add them all up and PRESTO, you have the figure to send to your accountant. At each reporting period, the accountant will add the work in process figure you just gave him and subtract the figure you gave him for the previous period. This will result in a balance sheet and profit and loss statement with the highest degree of accuracy that you need.

Now, there is an even quicker, easier although slightly less accurate method for figuring work in process. Here is how you do it. In chapter 11 you learned how to calculate an average hourly total cost. In our sample that cost was $27.28. Using that figure for the sake of learning this process, turn to the job cost record, add up the total number of man-hours invested in the job to date and multiply that total by $27.28. The product of that multiplication will be the labor cost to date. Add to that any cost for material and/or subcontract and you will have the value of the work in process for the job. This is not as accurate as the previously described method because it assumes that the average hourly cost on this job is the same as it is for all the jobs, which may not be the case but it is very often accurate enough.

CHAPTER 16

MANAGEMENT SKILLS
·····································

1. Cost estimating. Since chapter six described how to go about cost estimating, there is no further need to describe that, but the management of cost estimating is too often ignored, resulting in a lot of wasted time. The manager has to decide which jobs to bid on and it is a good idea to have a predetermined set of priorities to help you in making those decisions. Priorities could be listed like this, for instance;

#1. Any requests for bids from your best and most frequent customers.

#2. Requests for bids from good but less frequent customers.

#3. Requests for bids from businesses or individuals whom you would like to have for customers.

#4. Unsolicited quotes you give to potential customers who may not know you. This is commonly done in bidding public jobs.

If you have an estimator other than yourself, make sure that he or she knows your priorities. Your estimator will lose respect for you if he does an estimate and you do not bid the job, simply because of poor planning on your part.

2. Central office organization.

Back in chapter four you learned what basic files you need. Now we'll discuss relations between the people who use the office. If yours is more than a one person business, then you must clearly define what each person's job is. I suggest that you agree upon and write up each person's job description. Whenever one encroaches on another's area of responsibility, if it creates a problem, a simple referral to the job descriptions should serve as a reminder.

Often certain duties are included in the job description of more than one officer.

Relations with customers, for instance, have to be everyone's responsibility. Getting bills out in a timely manner should be done by one person so that it is done consistently the same way each time. Dunning customers for money should be one person's job likewise for the same reason. One partner's painstaking leading of a debtor into a systematic payment schedule could have his work ruined by another partner's threat of litigation to the same customer.

3. Production organization.

Most contractors find very early that they cannot supervise all of their jobs personally and full time. They also learn that if they leave the jobs unsupervised, the jobs lose money. Thus they must delegate the work of supervision to others, generally known as foremen. A foreman should be experienced in the trade, mature, sensible, and reliable. He or she should be paid more than comparably skilled and knowledgeable painters who are not expected to lead jobs. The foreman needs certain information from you in order to best perform the job of foremanship. This information can be summarized as "What work is supposed to be done". This is best defined for him on paper so that he can refer to it from time to time as needed. The estimating recapitulation (plate 10)

PLATE 10

JOB *Milford Library Addition*   **BID DUE DATE** *6/28/05*

ARCHITECT *Argeault*   **PHONE** *(508) 865 6800*

OWNER *city of Milford*   **SECTION** *09900*   **ADDENDA** *1, 2*

POSTED PAY SCALE *$ 20.07*   **COST PER HOUR** *$ 40.00*

HRS	SUBSTRATE AND PROCESS	QUAN	LUC	MUC	TUC	EXT
42	conc. block, blockfill & 1 coat epoxy	3290 SF	.51	.21	.72	2369
12	new hollow metal jambs two coats enamel	16	30.00	1.00	31.00	496
19	flush wood doors, stain, two coats clear	19	40.00	2.00	42.00	798
3	paint backstops one coat	3 hrs	40.00	2.00	42.00	126
5	contingencies	5 hrs	40.00		40.00	200
7	setup, cleanout, travel	7 hrs	40.00		40.00	280
88	**TOTALS**					3263

PROFIT   *297*

PRICE   *3550*

NOTES *Work expected to be done in July*

QUALIFICATION OF BID *Pavement marking not included even tho it is specified in section 0990*

form is a must because it tells him the scope of the work and the number of hours of labor you have estimated will be needed to do each substrate. If you do not want him to be privy to your dollar estimates of cost or to your estimated profit, simply cut off or blank out those portions of the recap and provide the foreman with the rest of it. If you expect the foreman to order paint as the job progresses, then also give him the estimating work sheets (plate 8) also. These will show him how much surface will be painted and help him to order the right amount of material. The estimating work sheets also give him a complete list of things to be done and tell him or her where in the building the work is located.

For jobs which are designed and specified by an architect, be sure to give your foreman a set of plans and specifications plus any specific instructions you may have for him about how you want the job to be run. An unscrupulous construction superintendent might well take advantage of a trade foreman who is ignorant of the true scope of work required by his contract. Don't let your foreman get into a job without knowing what the contract requires. If you do, you might end up paying your painters to do extra work that you don't get paid for. On many occasions we have worked on new buildings with gypsum board walls and hollow metal door frames. The frames had to be caulked to the walls before painting. In one instance the architect's specifications clearly made that caulking the responsibility of the carpenters, but the construction superintendent (whose employer also paid the carpenters' wages) told our foreman to do it. He foolishly agreed to do so because it is common for painters to caulk, thus making a gift of labor and material to the customer. Beware of such accidental gifts.

Only you, the contractor, know how to allocate personnel each day. This function has to be done by you and has to be done early enough each work day to ensure that your painters arrive at their jobs on time. Nothing frustrates a customer more than to expect your crew to show up on a job site and for that not to happen. On some occasions, circumstances will prevent you from doing for your customer what you promised him. Make sure that those occasions are very rare and if they happen, make sure that you immediately contact the customer with an abject, groveling apology. Also go out of your way to make up for any loss you may have caused him by your failure. Remember who pays your bills.

On the other hand, do not send a crew ready to work solely on the customer's word that the job is ready for you. Check it yourself first. A great way to waste a lot of money on labor is to start a job which is not really ready for painting. Construction superintendents are always worrying about subcontractors not arriving early enough, so they habitually call in the subs before they are needed. You can avoid throwing some of your money down the sewer by visiting the job (and the "super") before you send in the painters. Such a visit to the job site does not offend the "super". On the contrary, it reassures him that he is dealing with a professional who takes his interests seriously.

All written communications must be not only be clear but they must say what you mean. Our business once took it on the chin with one customer because of careless wording of a quotation. The building to be repainted on the exterior was shown to us by the owner. It was too tall a structure for us to see the roof from the ground and the owner pointed out all the work he wanted done on walls. When we wrote the quotation, we should have described the scope of work as exterior walls but we didn't. We used the expression "exterior surfaces". The owner was a sharp merchant who loved a bargain so he made us paint all the rooftop equipment for nothing because it fell into the category of exterior surfaces. To make matters worse, he said that we need only supply equipment and labor and he would supply the materials. However our sloppily drawn quotation mentioned that the owner would supply "paint". This same clever little guy refused to pay for the solvents because our contract only required him to provide "paint", rather than all materials as he originally intended. Naturally, you have no doubt all ready figured out that it was a spray job, the paint was epoxy, and the solvent was horrendously expensive and we had to use a lot of it to clean the spray equipment each day.

Our letter quoting the job, which became the basis of the contract, was clear all right. It just did not say what it meant. Since any document can be used in court, make all documents truly represent what you wish them to convey.

Bids must show prices, naturally, but they should also clearly define the scope and specifications of the work being bid. Some times it is easiest to list what you do not include in your price. For example, if you are quoting a repaint of a wooden building's exterior, and the building has painted trim, doors, and windows and stained siding, and the customer wants only the trim, windows, and doors repainted, a simple statement that all exterior woodwork is included except siding, would clearly delineate the scope of your bid. In fact, it is a very good idea to have one or two bid forms made up which you can fill out when bidding. These forms act as a checklist to make sure that you really include everything you need to say. If you do this, make sure that one space on the form is titled "EXCLUSIONS".

If you write a letter to a customer when you are very angry at him, by all means write whatever pops into your head but DO NOT MAIL IT until the next day. By that time you may decide to do a little rewording.

When you send out bills, make sure they include all of this stuff; 1. date (natch) 2. number of bill (you need this, even if the customer does not) 3. your job identification as well as the customer's 4. The customer's correct name and address

5. description of the work being billed 6. amount of the bill 7. terms of payment (this is often printed on the billhead).

The reason for #4 above is for legal protection. A customer who has decided to defraud; you can easily and legally ignore a bill that is not meticulously correct in his name and address.

One last word on office organization. NEVER DISCARD A DOCUMENT. Even scribbled notes can help you later when you need evidence to remind you what you said or did, or what your customer said or did. Keep all these things in your job folders forever (well, seven years anyway).

CHAPTER 17

EPILOGUE
....

Every author drools over the prospect of putting his dreams on paper and then having somebody actually read them, and since this is my book and I have to end it some way, I hereby do some last minute musing. I dream of a greatly improved painting industry in this country. We have allowed it to deteriorate to, at best, a semi-profession. I believe the cause of this deterioration is the demise of the discipline provided in the past by strong trade guilds (organizations of contractors) and strong labor unions. Some countries, Germany for example, have such organizations and thus have a more professional painting industry than we have. In Germany the contractors and the unions are willing to accept that some of their interests actually coincide. Therefore they approach all issues on the basis of cooperation rather than the acrimonious enmity so prevalent in America.

I have seen shlock contractors destroy the public's faith in the building trades through shady dealings, unreliable service and poor workmanship. I have seen shlock unions kill the goose which should have kept on laying the golden egg. They did this by applying their overwhelming power over the disorganized contractors and driving wages up too high for the market to bear. The great melt down of the building trades unions in the AFL-CIO in the nineteen seventies and eighties and the serious increase in numbers of shoddy contractors in the same time period attest to the lack of disciplinary forces on both union and management sides.

When I signed my first union collective bargaining agreement in 1957, I did so with some trepidation because I had no experience with union help and did not know what to expect. Until that time, my best painter employee was earning $1.80 per hour and the union rate for journeymen was $2.50. My guy could and would have been earning $2.50 but for two factors which inhibited him. One was his health. He had a bad heart and could not do strenuous work. The other was his choice not to learn spray painting. For that reason, I assumed that $2.50 was a fair rate for skilled, experienced painters. I learned that this was true after only a few weeks of using only union help. I was very happy as a union contractor for seventeen of the twenty years I stuck with the union. The supply of help was reliable and the quality of the help was good. What eventually drove me out of the collective bargaining agreement was a change in attitude in the local union. It became very greedy and drove wages so high that contractors could not make it any more. They either went out of business entirely or went non-union. At present, there are, to the best of my knowledge, no union contractors left in a city that formerly had approximately two dozen.

The national union did nothing to stop the local's feeding frenzy and the local PDCA chapter was too weak to take a unified stand against the union. The result was what we now have; lots of small, financially weak, inexperienced contractors, and a small, financially weak, inexperienced local union. We have no local contractors' organization at all.

We need a strong national PDCA and a strong AFL-CIO with both sides willing to keep some disciplinary control over their local chapters and unions and willing to look at all labor-management issues in a cooperative manner. We must realize that, in most issues, both sides have the same interests.

Enough said, perhaps. To those of you who had the guts to wade through this whole book, I say, good luck in business. If you wish to contact me for help, my e-mail address is arthurcole1@verizon.net.

ILLUSTRATIONS

PLATES 1 AND 2

CURVED SIDE STAINED AND VARNISHED

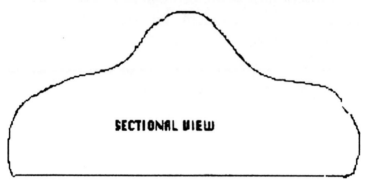

SECTIONAL VIEW

FLAT SIDE PAINTED

1	2	3
4	5	6
7	8	9

PLATE 13

JOB *27 Ripon Street*   **BID DUE DATE** *4/16/04*

ARCHITECT   **PHONE**

OWNER *John Somers*   **SECTION**   **ADDENDA**

POSTED PAY SCALE   **COST PER HOUR** *30.00*

HOURS	PROCESS	QUAN	LUC	MUC	EXT
733	*LABOR*	*733 HRS*	*26.00*		*21,990*
	MATERIALS, PAINT, ETC.				*450*
30	*CONTINGENCIES*	*30 HR*	*S26.00*		*900*
	WALLPAPER (SUPPLIED BY OWNER)				
	TOTALS				*23,340*

PROFIT   *2,300*

PRICE   *26,640*

PLATE 4

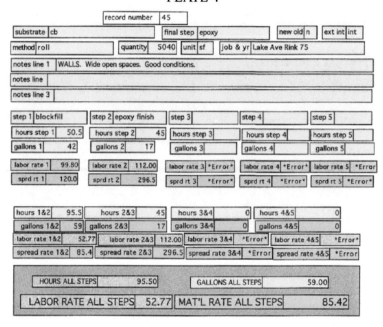

record number	45

substrate	cb		final step	epoxy		new old	n	ext int	int

method	roll		quantity	5040	unit	sf	job & yr	Lake Ave Rink 75

notes line 1	WALLS. Wide open spaces. Good conditions.
notes line	
notes line 3	

step 1	blockfill	step 2	epoxy finish	step 3		step 4		step 5	
hours step 1	50.5	hours step 2	45	hours step 3		hours step 4		hours step 5	
gallons 1	42	gallons 2	17	gallons 3		gallons 4		gallons 5	
labor rate 1	99.80	labor rate 2	112.00	labor rate 3	*Error*	labor rate 4	*Error*	labor rate 5	*Error*
sprd rt 1	120.0	sprd rt 2	296.5	sprd rt 3	*Error*	sprd rt 4	*Error*	sprd rt 5	*Error*

hours 1&2	95.5	hours 2&3	45	hours 3&4	0	hours 4&5	0
gallons 1&2	59	gallons 2&3	17	gallons 3&4	0	gallons 4&5	0
labor rate 1&2	52.77	labor rate 2&3	112.00	labor rate 3&4	*Error*	labor rate 4&5	*Error*
spread rate 1&2	85.4	spread rate 2&3	296.5	spread rate 3&4	*Error*	spread rate 4&5	*Error*

HOURS ALL STEPS	95.50	GALLONS ALL STEPS	59.00
LABOR RATE ALL STEPS	52.77	MAT'L RATE ALL STEPS	85.42

PLATE 5

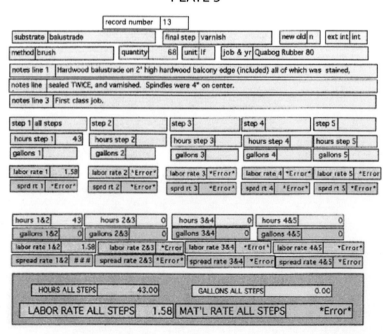

record number	13

substrate	balustrade		final step	varnish		new old	n	ext int	int

method	brush		quantity	68	unit	lf	job & yr	Quabog Rubber 80

notes line 1	Hardwood balustrade on 2' high hardwood balcony edge (included) all of which was stained,
notes line	sealed TWICE, and varnished. Spindles were 4" on center.
notes line 3	First class job.

step 1	all steps	step 2		step 3		step 4		step 5	
hours step 1	43	hours step 2		hours step 3		hours step 4		hours step 5	
gallons 1		gallons 2		gallons 3		gallons 4		gallons 5	
labor rate 1	1.58	labor rate 2	*Error*	labor rate 3	*Error*	labor rate 4	*Error*	labor rate 5	*Error*
sprd rt 1	*Error*	sprd rt 2	*Error*	sprd rt 3	*Error*	sprd rt 4	*Error*	sprd rt 5	*Error*

hours 1&2	43	hours 2&3	0	hours 3&4	0	hours 4&5	0
gallons 1&2	0	gallons 2&3	0	gallons 3&4	0	gallons 4&5	0
labor rate 1&2	1.58	labor rate 2&3	*Error*	labor rate 3&4	*Error*	labor rate 4&5	*Error*
spread rate 1&2	###	spread rate 2&3	*Error*	spread rate 3&4	*Error*	spread rate 4&5	*Error*

HOURS ALL STEPS	43.00	GALLONS ALL STEPS	0.00
LABOR RATE ALL STEPS	1.58	MAT'L RATE ALL STEPS	*Error*

PLATE 6

record number	336	

substrate	sm surf		final step	paint		new old	o	ext int	int
method	spray		quantity	16000	unit	sf	job & yr	Mary Chapel, HC 82	

notes line 1	WALLS AND CEILINGS together in vaulted chapel. Pews, floors, statues, fixtures
notes line	masked first. Major masking job. It cost $626 for masking materials. Plaster patching
notes line 3	was major enough to subcontract, therefore not included here.

step 1	Mask & cover.	step 2	wash		step 3	prime		step 4	intermediate	step 5	finish
hours step 1	101.5	hours step 2	16.5	hours step 3	30	hours step 4	29	hours step 5	29
gallons 1		gallons 2		gallons 3	50	gallons 4	60	gallons 5	60
labor rate 1	157.64	labor rate 2	969.70	labor rate 3	533.33	labor rate 4	551.72	labor rate 5	551.72
sprd rt 1	*Error*	sprd rt 2	*Error*	sprd rt 3	320.0	sprd rt 4	266.67	sprd rt 5	266.7

hours 1&2	118	hours 2&3	46.5	hours 3&4	59	hours 4&5	58
gallons 1&2	0	gallons 2&3	50	gallons 3&4	110	gallons 4&5	120
labor rate 1&2	135.59	labor rate 2&3	344.09	labor rate 3&4	271.19	labor rate 4&5	275.86
spread rate 1&2	###	spread rate 2&3	320.0	spread rate 3&4	145.5	spread rate 4&5	133.3

HOURS ALL STEPS	206.00	GALLONS ALL STEPS	170.00
LABOR RATE ALL STEPS	77.67	MAT'L RATE ALL STEPS	94.12

PLATE 7

			PAGE	1 OF	1	JOB	Simpson			SUBSTRATE				
										GWB ptd	conc. Floor	oak trim	door refin.	jamb ptd.
AREA	L	W	H	OUTS	WALL	TRIM	CL'G	FLOOR						
lobby	20	20	9		x	x				720		80		
men	8	10	8	4' dado	x	x	x	x		144+80	80			
auditorium	32	44	10		x	x				1520			8	6
all														
TOTALS										2464	80	80	8	6

PLATE 8

	A	B	C	D	E	F	G	H	I	K	L	M	N	O	P
1				PAGE		1 OF		1 JOB	Arcon Plastics						
3													SUBSTRATE		
5	AREA	L	W	H		OUTS	WALL	TRIM	CL'G FLOOR	brick pt'd	CB pt'd	window	jamb	rib deck	
7	north	100		25	150sf	x				2350		20			
8	east	50		25	50sf	x		x			1200	7	1	200	
9	south	100		25		x				2500		15			
10	west	50		25		x				1250		7	2		
11															
12															
13															
18															
19															
20															
21															
22															
23															
24															
25															
26															
27															
28															
29															
30															
31															
32															
33															
34															
35															
36															
37															
38															
39															
40															
41															
43				TOTALS						6100	1200	49	3	200	

PLATE 9

A B	C	D	E	F
1 INFORMATION FOR FUN & PROFIT	DESCRIPTION	**3dYEAR**	**2dYEAR**	**1st YEAR**
2 YOU FILL IN THE FIGURES		**1993**	**1992**	**1991**
3 GROSS INCOME	TOTAL SALES	510345	465321	401291
4 SALARIES	FIXED OVERHEAD	42000	42000	42000
5 **INTEREST LONG TERM**	FIXED OVERHEAD	1000	1200	1500
6 FICA EXECUTIVES	FIXED OVERHEAD	3213	3213	3213
7 ALL INSURANCE COSTS, EXECUTIVES	FIXED OVERHEAD	2389	2341	2310
8 TELEPHONE AND ADVERTISING	FIXED OVERHEAD	4131	3810	4501
9 CHARITABLE DONATIONS	FIXED OVERHEAD	250	300	225
10 ENTERTAINMENT	FIXED OVERHEAD	100		
11 VEHICLE MAINTENANCE	FIXED OVERHEAD	2748	1745	1528
12 VEHICLE LICENSE AND INSURANCE	FIXED OVERHEAD	2800	2900	3210
13 VEHICLE DEPRECIATION	FIXED OVERHEAD	2200	2900	3400
14 EAQUIPMENT DEPRECIATION	FIXED OVERHEAD	3900	4200	4500
15 EQUIPMENT INSURANCE	FIXED OVERHEAD	650	650	650
16 SHOP RENT, UTILITIES, AND TAXES	FIXED OVERHEAD	7000	6950	5950
17 DEPREC., LEASEHOLD IMPROVEMENTS	FIXED OVERHEAD		500	500
18 OFFICE EXPENSE	FIXED OVERHEAD	2243	1937	1866
19 LEGAL AND AUDIT EXPENSE	FIXED OVERHEAD	310	310	659
20 DUES AND SUBSCRIPTIONS	FIXED OVERHEAD	150	150	150
21 MISCELLANEOUS EXPENSE	FIXED OVERHEAD	1322	1111	997
22 TOTAL GENERAL OVERHEAD	all above fixed overhead	76404	76217	78249
23 TOTAL HOURS ESTIMATING	self explanatory	1580	1784	1649
24 WAGE COST FOR ESTIMATING	FIXED OVERHEAD	18100	21408	20365
25 WORKERS' COMP., ESTIMATING	FIXED OVERHEAD	1810	2141	2037
26 LIABILITY INSURANCE, ESTIMATING	FIXED OVERHEAD	805	1019	999
27 FICA, ESTIMATING	FIXED OVERHEAD	1424	1638	1558
28 UNEMPLOYMENT INS., ESTIMATING	FIXED OVERHEAD	905	1019	999
29 HEALTH INSURANCE, ESTIMATING	FIXED OVERHEAD	1230	1123	1067
30 TOTAL COST, ESTIMATING	total above 6 lines	24274	28348	27025
31 COST PER HOUR, ESTIMATING	mean	15.36	15.89	16.39
32 TOTAL FIXED OVERHEAD FOR YEAR	**grand total fixed o/h**	**100678**	**104385**	**105274**
33 OTHER NONPRODUCTIVE HOURS (ONPH)	down time hours	798	508	591
34 WAGE COST ONPH	VARIABLE OVERHEAD	9100	5080	5781
35 WORKERS' COMP., ONPH	VARIABLE OVERHEAD	910	506	578
36 LIABILITY INSURANCE, ONPH	VARIABLE OVERHEAD	455	254	289
37 FICA ONPH	VARIABLE OVERHEAD	896	389	442
38 UNEMPLOYMENT INS., ONPH	VARIABLE OVERHEAD	455	508	578
39 HEALTH INSURANCE, ONPH	VARIABLE OVERHEAD	810	736	821
40 TOTAL COST, ONPH	total above 6 lines	12228	7475	8489
41 COST/HOUR, ONPH	mean	15.32	14.71	14.36
42 TOTAL PRODUCTIVE HOURS FOR YEAR	direct hours on jobs	13121	11377	10002
43 WAGE COST, PRODUCTIVE HOURS	DIRECT COST	162589	135273	114023
44 WORKERS' COMP., PRODUCTIVE HOURS	VARIABLE OVERHEAD	16259	13527	11402
45 LIABILITY INS., PRODUCTIVE HOURS	VARIABLE OVERHEAD	8130	8764	5701
46 FICA, PRODUCTIVE HOURS	VARIABLE OVERHEAD	12438	10348	8123
47 UNEMPLOYMENT INS., PROD. HOURS	VARIABLE OVERHEAD	8130	8764	5701
48 HEALTH INS., PRODUCTIVE HOURS	VARIABLE OVERHEAD	13705	11002	9399
49 **INTEREST SHORT TERM**	VARIABLE OVERHEAD	3122	2000	1348
50 HAZARDOUS WASTE	VARIABLE OVERHEAD	2911	2142	1311
51 EQUIPMENT MAINTENANCE	VARIABLE OVERHEAD	997	137	429
52 SMALL TOOL EXPENSE	VARIABLE OVERHEAD	18756	14333	10492
53 SUM OF TWO PRIOR LINES	often useful subtotal	17753	14470	10921
54 PRIOR LINE COST/PRODUCTIVE HOUR	often useful ratio	1.35	1.27	1.09
55 TOTAL VARIABLE OVERHEAD, YEAR	**VARIABLE OVERHEAD**	**94674**	**74493**	**63495**
56 VARIABLE O/H PER PRODUCTIVE HOUR	at mean hourly wage	7.22	6.55	6.35
57 FIXED O/H PER PRODUCTIVE HOUR	at any wage level	7.67	9.17	10.53
58 WAGES PER PRODUCTIVE HOUR	at mean hourly wage	12.39	11.89	11.40
59 TOTAL COST PER PRODUCTIVE HOUR	**at mean hourly wage**	**27.28**	**27.61**	**28.27**
60 DOLLAR SALES PER PRODUCTIVE HOUR	interesting but useless	38.9	40.9	40.12
61 VARIABLE O/H AS % OF WAGES	vital information	58.20%	55.10%	55.70%
62 LINE 61 LESS LINE 53	useful in pricing overtime	47.30%	44.40%	46.10%

PLATE 10

JOB *Milford Library Addition*   **BID DUE DATE** *6/28/05*

ARCHITECT *Argeault*   **PHONE** *(508) 865 6800*

OWNER *city of Milford*   **SECTION** *09900*   **ADDENDA** *1, 2*

POSTED PAY SCALE *$ 20.07*   **COST PER HOUR** *$ 40.00*

HRS	SUBSTRATE AND PROCESS	QUAN	LUC	MUC	TUC	EXT
42	conc. block, blockfill & 1 coat epoxy	3290 SF	.51	.21	.72	2369
12	new hollow metal jambs two coats enamel	16	30.00	1.00	31.00	496
19	flush wood doors, stain, two coats clear	19	40.00	2.00	42.00	798
3	paint backstops one coat	3 hrs	40.00	2.00	42.00	126
5	contingencies	5 hrs	40.00		40.00	200
7	setup, cleanout, travel	7 hrs	40.00		40.00	280
88	**TOTALS**					3263

PROFIT   297

PRICE   3550

NOTES *Work expected to be done in July*

QUALIFICATION OF BID *Pavement marking not included even tho it is specified in section 0990*

PLATE 11

JOB NAME	SUN	MON	TUE	WED	THU	FRI	SAT	S/T HRS	O/T HRS	ALL HRS	$ COST
Smith		8	3	1				12		12	120.00
Jones			7	8				15		15	150.00
Newton						6		6		6	60.00
Abstract					2				2	2	30.00
Williams						3		2	1	3	35.00
no job (onph)			5					5		5	50.00
TOTALS		8	8	8	10	9		40	3	43	445.00

PLATE 12

INFORMATION FOR FUN AND PROFIT	DESCRIPTION	FORMULAS USED
GROSS INCOME	TOTAL SALES	
EXECUTIVE SALARIES	fixed overhead	
INTEREST LONG TERM	fixed overhead	
FICA, EXECUTIVES	fixed overhead	=D4*.0675
EXECS	fixed overhead	
ADVERTISING	fixed overhead	
CHARITY DONATIONS	fixed overhead	
ENTERTAINMENT	fixed overhead	
VEHICLE MAINTENANCE	fixed overhead	
VEHICLE LICENSE, INSURANCE	fixed overhead	
VEHICLE DEPRECIATION	fixed overhead	
DEPRECIATION	fixed overhead	
EQUIPMENT INSURANCE	fixed overhead	
SHOP RENT, UTILITIES, TAXES	fixed overhead	
DEPRECIATION OF LEASEHOLD IMPROVEMENTS	fixed overhead	
OFFICE EXPENSES	fixed overhead	
LEGAL AND AUDIT EXPENSE	fixed overhead	
DUES AND SUBSCRIPTIONS	fixed overhead	
MISCELLANEOUS EXPENSE	fixed overhead	
TOTAL GENERAL OVERHEAD		=SUM(D4:D21)

ESTIMATING		
WAGES, ESTIMATING	fixed overhead	
ESTIMATING	fixed overhead	
ESTIMATING	fixed overhead	
FICA ESTIMATING	fixed overhead	=D24*.0675
UNEMPLOYMENT INS. ESTIMATING	fixed overhead	
HEALTH INS. ESTIMATING	fixed overhead	
TOTAL COST ESTIMATING	fixed overhead	=SUM(D24:D29)
COST/HOUR ESTIMATING		=D30/D23
TOTAL FIXED OVERHEAD FOR THE YEAR		=SUM(D22+D30)
OTHER NON-PRODUCTIVE HOURS (ONPH)	down time hours	
WAGES, ONPH	variable overhead	
WORKERS COMP ONPH	variable overhead	
LIABILITY INS. ONPH	variable overhead	
FICA ONPH	variable overhead	=D34*.0765
ONPH	variable overhead	
HEALTH INS. ONPH	variable overhead	
TOTAL COST ONPH	variable overhead	=SUM(D34:D39)
COST PER HOUR ONPH		=D40/D33
TOTAL PRODUCTIVE HOURS FOR THE YEAR	direct job labor	
WAGES, PRODUCTIVE HOURS	direct cost	
WORKERS COMP, PRODUCTIVE HOURS	variable overhead	
LIABILITY INS., PRODUCTIVE HOURS	variable overhead	
FICA, PRODUCTIVE HOURS	variable overhead	=D43*.0765
UNEMPLOYMENT INS. PRODUCTIVE HOURS	variable overhead	
HEALTH INS. PRODUCTIVE HOURS	variable overhead	
INTEREST, SHORT TERM	variable overhead	
HAZARDOUS WASTE	variable overhead	
EQUIPMENT MAINTENANCE	variable overhead	
SMALL TOOL EXPENSE	variable overhead	

SUM OF TWO PRIOR LINES	useful subtotal	
TOOLS & EQUIP. MAINT. PER PRODUCTIVE HOUR	useful ratio	=D53/D42
TOTAL VARIABLE OVERHEAD FOR THE YEAR	variable overhead	=D40+SUM(D44:D52)
VARIABLE OVERHEAD PER PRODUCTIVE HOUR	at average wage	=D55/D42
FIXED OVERHEAD PER PRODUCTIVE HOUR	fixed overhead	=D32/D42
WAGES PER PRODUCTIVE HOUR	average wage	=D43/D42
TOTAL COST PER PRODUCTIVE HOUR	at average wage	=SUM(D56:D58)
DOLLAR SALES PER PRODUCTIVE HOUR	interesting ratio	=D3/D42
VARIABLE OVERHEAD AS A PERCENT OF WAGES	vital information	=D55/D43
LINE 61 LESS LINE 53	useful for pricing overtime work	=(D55-D53)/D43

PLATE 13

JOB *27 Ripon Street*   **BID DUE DATE** *4/16/04*

ARCHITECT   **PHONE**

OWNER *John Somers*   **SECTION**   **ADDENDA**

POSTED PAY SCALE   **COST PER HOUR** *30.00*

HOURS	PROCESS	QUAN	LUC	MUC	EXT
733	*LABOR*	*733 HRS*	*26.00*		*21,990*
	MATERIALS, PAINT, ETC.				*450*
30	*CONTINGENCIES*	*30 HR*	*S 26.00*		*900*
	WALLPAPER (SUPPLIED BY OWNER)				
	TOTALS				*23,340*

                              PROFIT   *2,300*

                              PRICE   *26,640*

PLATE 14

JOB COST RECAP BASED ON OVERHEAD OF YEAR *1993*

Total Hours labor *54* X $ *7.67* (fixed overhead)	*414.18*
Total direct wages	*660.00*
Direct wages X *58%* (variable overhead)	*382.80*
Subcontract expense	*2500.00*
Material expense	*38.92*
TOTAL COST (SUM OF LINES ABOVE)	*3995.80*
Total Amount Billed	*4200.00*
NET PROFIT OR (LOSS)	*204.20*

PLATE 16

WEEKLY PAYROLL RECAP

WEEK ENDING _____

EMPLOYEE	HOURS WORKED	GROSS PAY	ONPH HRS.	ONPH $	EST'G HRS.	EST'G $	Smith job HOURS	Smith job $	Jones job HOURS	Jones job $	Newton job HOURS	Newton job$	Abstract job HOURS	Abstract job $	Williams job HOURS	Williams job $
Trainor, W.	4	$600.00		$540.00									4	$60.00		
jackson, F.	40	$500.00	4	$50.00	13	$162.50					23	$287.50				
Ruiz, P.	43	$445.00	5	$50.00			12	$120.00	15	$150.00	6	$60.00	2	$30.00	3	$35.00
Nelson, H.	39	$507.00					4.5	$58.50	14.5	$188.50	20	$260.00				
Ricker, O.	40	$480.00													40	$480.00
TOTALS	166	$2,532.00	9	$640.00	13	$162.50	16.5	$178.50	29.5	$338.50	49	$607.50	6	$90.00	43	$515.00

PLATE 18

WEEKLY PAYROLL RECAP

WEEK ENDING _____

PAYROLL RECAPITULATION WEEK ENDING _____

EMPLOYEE	HOURS WORKED	GROSS PAY	ONPH HRS.	ONPH $	ESTG HRS.	ESTG $	Smith Job HOURS	Smith Job $	Jones Job HOURS	Jones Job $	Newton Job HOURS	Newton Job $	Abstract Job HOURS	Abstract Job $	Williams Job HOURS	Williams Job $
Trainor	40	$720.00	-2	$36.00	26	$468.00							16	$288.00		
Jackson, F	40	$500.00	5	$50.00	26	$325.00							1	$12.50	3	$35.00
Ruiz, P	43	$445.00					12	$120.00	15	$150.00	13	$162.50	2	$30.00		
Nelson, H	39	$507.00					4.5	$58.50	14.5	$188.50	6	$60.00				
Ricker, O	40	$480.00									20	$260.00			40	$490.00
TOTALS	202	$2,652.00	3	$14.00	52	$793.00	16.5	$178.50	29.5	$338.50	39	$482.50	19	$330.50	43	$515.00

PLATE 17

JOB_____REG. #_____C. S. PAGE____
SALES TAX EXEMPT #_____
COST PLUS_____CONTRACT_____CONTRACT PRICE
$_____

LABOR			SUBCONTRACT			MATERIAL		
date	am't	hrs.	date	name	am't	date	name	am't
		frd			frd			frd
	frd	frd			frd			frd

REQUISITIONS				PAYMENTS RECEIVED				
date	amount	date	amount	date	amount	date	amount

PLATE 19

JOB _Jones_____REG. #__3386_____C. S. PAGE_1
SALES TAX EXEMPT #_____
COST PLUS_____CONTRACT_x___CONTRACT PRICE
$_4,200_____

LABOR			SUBCONTRACT			MATERIAL		
date	am't	hrs.	date	name	am't	date	name	am't
		frd			frd			frd
6/15	612.00	51	6/18	Atlas Sand	2500.00	6/10	Glidden	38.92
6/22	48.00	3		Blasting				
	frd	frd			frd			frd
	660.00	54			2500.0			38.92

REQUISITIONS

PAYMENTS RECEIVED

date	amount	date	amount	date	amount	date	amout
7/10	4200.00			8/1	1450.00		
				8/10	2750.00		
					4200.00		

PLATE 20

YOUR BUSINESS NAME
STATEMENT OF INCOME FOR THE YEAR ENDING 12/31/1993

SALES		510,345
COST OF SALES (direct costs)		
Materials	100,766	
Subcontracts	34,907	
Direct Labor	189,789	
FICA (social security)	14,518	
State Unemployment Insurance	6,324	
Federal Unemployment Insurance	451	
Depreciation	4,288	
Workers' Compensation Insurance	19,587	
General Liability Insurance	3.010	
Equipment Rental	4,000	
TOTAL COST OF SALES		377,640
GROSS PROFIT		132,705
OPERATING EXPENSES (overhead)		
Officers' salaries	42,000	
FICA, officers	3,213	
Workers' Compensation, officers	2,033	
Motor Vehicle Insurance	2,900	
Health Insurance	6,933	
Profit Sharing	3,800	
Interest	4,122	
Motor Vehicle maintenance and fuel	2,746	
Shop and Office Rent	6.500	
Legal and Accounting Expense	3,100	
Telephone	1,247	
Advertising	2,884	
Equipment Maintenance	997	
Dues and Subscriptions	350	
Small Tool Expense	1,568	

Miscellaneous General Expense	16,756
Hazardous Waste Removal	5,980
TOTAL OPERATIONAL EXPENSES	104,245
NET PROFIT OR (LOSS)	28,460

PLATE 21

BALANCE SHEET AS OF DECEMBER 31, 2011

ASSETS

CURRENT ASSETS

Cash	$ 6,123.65
Accounts Receivable	71,954.77
Work in Process	3,996.00
TOTAL	$ 82,074.42

FIXED ASSETS

Equipment	$ 20,675.00
Furniture and Fixtures	1,850.45
Motor Vehicles	23,053.06
Less Accumulated Depreciation	(12,371.00)
TOTAL	$ 33,207.51
TOTAL ASSETS	$ 115,281.93

LIABILITIES AND CAPITAL

CURRENT LIABILITIES

Accounts Payable	$ 33,671.98
Accrued Taxes and Expenses	3,456.00
Notes Payable	24,000.00
TOTAL	$61,127.98

CAPITAL

Common Stock 600 shares	$ 18,000.00
Retained Earnings	36,153.93
TOTAL	$ 54,153.95
TOTAL LIABILITIES AND CAPITAL	$ 115,281.93

PLATE 22

DATE RECEIVED_____

JOB_____ $_____

JOB_____ $_____

JOB_____ $_____

SMALL TOOLS $_____

OTHER ACC'T _____ $_____

CHECKED BY_____AP#_____

COST SHEET ENTRY BY_____

PAID CHK #_____DATE_____

PLATE 23

JOB   **BID DUE DATE**

ARCHITECT   **PHONE**

OWNER   **SECTION**   **ADDENDA**

POSTED PAY SCALE   **COST PER HOUR** *$26.00*

HRS	SUBSTRATE	PROCESS	QUAN	U	LPR	MSR	MC/G	LUC	MUC	TUC	EXT
13.4	conc block	2 coats flat latex rolled	2340	sf	175	200	14.50	0.149	0.072	0.221	517
12.0	hm jambs, new	2 coats enamel brushed	16	ea	1.33	9	24.00	19.549	2.667	22.216	355
16.0	flush wood drs	stain, seal, and 2 varnish	16	ea	1	7	20.00	26.000	2.857	28.857	462
48.8	smooth plaster	2 coats latex flat rolled	10986	sf	225	190	14.50	0.115	0.076	0.192	2106
12.0		staging & contingencies	12	hrs	1			26.000		26.000	312
102		TOTALS									3754

30736204R00100

Made in the USA
San Bernardino, CA
28 March 2019